"Bitingly funny . . . We follow w] sure where the story will end up b.. of such sharp-eyed dramatic intelligence."

— CHARLES MCNULTY, *LA TIMES*

"Mr. Jacobs-Jenkins brings an anthropological accuracy to his depiction of the hierarchies, language, and rites of obeisance and humiliation in one small, intensely stratified world . . . A straightforward, sharp-toothed comic drama."

— BEN BRANTLEY, *NEW YORK TIMES*

"A darkly comic masterpiece . . . A blistering satire, *Gloria* is a sharp, shrewd work that is bound to be a classic, and a chance to see one of the most skilled writers of our day at the height of his powers."

— TIM SULLIVAN, *BROADWAY WORLD*

"Cunningly structured . . . the play has powerful things to say about how we tune in and tune out."

— ADAM FELDMAN, *TIME OUT NEW YORK*

"A shocking, hilarious and spectacularly honest play . . . *Gloria* is a great roar of truth-telling, keenly observed, self-critical, and yet voiced with schadenfreude. You'll be gripped."

— CHRIS JONES, *CHICAGO TRIBUNE*

"Harshly funny . . . If you relish daring, smartly written theater that digs into the pith of contemporary American culture, you'll be positively blown away by Branden Jacobs-Jenkins's harrowing workplace drama . . . *Gloria* is an intellectually rich piece of writing full of ideas about personal narrative, media-driven desensitization, and mental health . . . A must-see."

— JIM GLADSTONE, *BAY AREA REPORTER*

"Sharply observant and playfully theatrical, this thought-provoking work continues its talented young writer's winning streak . . . As usual, the playwright handles his serious themes in a thoughtful, provocative manner . . . A trenchant commentary on the way in which personal tragedies merely serve as grist for the ever-ravenous media machine. A rare example of a contemporary play that keeps us constantly guessing where it's headed, *Gloria* is a work not to be easily forgotten."
— FRANK SCHECK, *HOLLYWOOD REPORTER*

"Branden Jacobs-Jenkins is one of America's boldest young playwrights."
— HENRY HITCHINGS, *EVENING STANDARD*

"Branden Jacobs-Jenkins is a playwright on a roll . . . The dialogue in *Gloria* tolls like a tuning fork and captures everyday interoffice insecurity . . . You never know what's going on at the water cooler and who's coming around the corner."
— JOE DZIEMIANOWICZ, *NEW YORK DAILY NEWS*

"A knockout play . . . Count on Branden Jacobs-Jenkins to leave you whiplashed and shell-shocked. He hits nerve after nerve then goes for the jugular. Whatever he writes, see it . . . Damn, that guy can write."
— JOE STOLTENBERG, *DC METRO THEATER ARTS*

"Branden Jacobs-Jenkins continues to be one of contemporary theater's most valuable assets. This is what theater should be: unique, sharp, funny, adventurous."
— HARVEY PERR, *STAGE AND CINEMA*

"Sometimes shocking, frequently hilarious . . . Jacobs-Jenkins's bitchy back-and-forth is hilariously specific to the early 2010s media industry . . . A crackling examination of office life . . . It's a play that offers you a lot to laugh about in the moment, and even more to discuss across your cubicle wall come Monday morning."
— JOHN BAVOSO, *DC THEATRE SCENE*

"Another goodie from Branden Jacobs-Jenkins . . . A fast-talking, cynical look at office politics and the culture of creative ambition . . . The dialogue is super-smart, crisply funny . . . *Gloria* is always sharply entertaining."

— Holly Williams, *Time Out London*

"The humor is dark and cruel, but terribly funny."

— Marilyn Stasio, *Variety*

"Crackles with familiarity . . . The dialogue is lightning fast, and it doesn't take long to suck us into the office drama involving secret manuscripts, the intern's last day and the frustrations of feeling that work is sucking all the life out of your life. There are barbs aimed at millennials and boomers, jealous tirades, and harsh confrontations, all before the lunch hour. But Jacobs-Jenkins has plans to go deeper into the office dynamic and what it means to share a formative experience with people who are neither friends nor family . . . Fascinating, funny, and frightening."

— Chad Jones, *Mercury News*

"*Gloria* takes a uniquely American look at how ego, privilege, and circumstance warp people's relationships with trauma and the telling of its story . . . *Gloria*'s arrival is timely . . . disquieting and devilishly enjoyable."

— Raphael Solarsh, *ArtsHub Australia*

"*Gloria* is a really, really good comedy. And it is a really, really good drama . . . *Gloria* holds up a mirror, whether you want it to or not . . . This is comedy with wit, bite, and fear . . . this is a show that creeps up on you."

— Mary Ann Johnson, *MD Theatre Guide*

"Brilliant . . . A biting, cynical black comedy . . . Jacobs-Jenkins proves himself a first-rate talent . . . A thought-provoking and boundary-pushing new work."

— Juliet Wittman, *Denver Westword*

"*Gloria* is a startling, vivid, densely layered experience. Branden Jacobs-Jenkins wraps mirth, mayhem, and petty office politics into the plot of *Gloria* . . . He artfully captures the frustration and ennui of this flat earth with its petty jealousies, dashed hopes, and long-nurtured grievances in crisp no-prisoners dialogue. It's all hysterically funny until suddenly, and quite shockingly, it isn't."

— ROBERT SOKOL, *SAN FRANCISCO EXAMINER*

"Brilliant . . . I've not seen a play in recent memory that has its finger more securely on the pulse of our crazy, unsettled times . . . This amazing play is not about the obvious. It is more about the tenor of the times, our sense of alienation and meaninglessness . . . Jacobs-Jenkins hits the bull's-eye with his searing sense of humor, offbeat imagery, and some of the freshest writing around . . . *Gloria* has it all: big views, virtuosic writing . . . A rare and wonderful night of theater."

— CHANNING GRAY, *PROVIDENCE JOURNAL*

"The play is darkly, observantly funny thanks to Jacobs-Jenkins's way with satire . . . In *Gloria*, Jacobs-Jenkins adroitly captures the zeitgeist of the contemporary workplace, the desire to be seen and appreciated, the psychological disconnect . . . Jacobs-Jenkins possesses a voice worth seeking out."

— CHRISTINE DOLEN, *MIAMI HERALD*

"Anyone who's ever worked in an office can probably relate to Branden Jacobs-Jenkins's *Gloria* . . . a smart, funny satire of the modern workplace . . . Thanks to the playwright's right-on dialogue we're highly entertained."

— KAY KIPLING, *SARASOTA MAGAZINE*

"Provocative . . . Clever, devious, and unrelenting, in equal measures."

— KATE WINGFIELD, *METRO WEEKLY*

"Branden Jacobs-Jenkins defies categorization . . . *Gloria* confounds expectation to a heady and exhilarating degree . . . *Gloria* is pretty glorious."

— MATT WOLF, *ARTS DESK*

GLORIA

GLORIA

BRANDEN JACOBS-JENKINS

THEATRE COMMUNICATIONS GROUP
NEW YORK
2020

Gloria is published by Theatre Communications Group, Inc.,
520 Eighth Avenue, 24th Floor, New York, NY 10018-4156

The publication of *Gloria* by Branden Jacobs-Jenkins, through TCG's Book Program, is made possible in part by the New York State Council on the Arts with the support of Governor Andrew Cuomo and the New York State Legislature.

TCG books are exclusively distributed to the book trade by Consortium Book Sales and Distribution.

Library of Congress Control Numbers:
2019020713 (print) / 2019021601 (ebook)
ISBN 978-1-55936-545-1 (trade paper) / ISBN 978-1-55936-866-7 (ebook)
A catalog record for this book is available from the Library of Congress.

Book design and composition by Lisa Govan
Cover design by Mark Melnick
Cover photographs: Ferran Traité (female portrait); Leonardo Patrizi (NYC night scene); Orbon Alija (NYC day scene)

First Edition, July 2020

GLORIA

Production History

Gloria received its world premiere at the Vineyard Theatre (Douglas Aibel and Sarah Stern, Artistic Directors) in New York on June 17, 2015. It was directed by Evan Cabnet. The set design was by Takeshi Kata, the costume design was by Ilona Somogyi, the lighting design was by Matt Frey, and the sound design was by Matt Tierney. The cast was:

DEAN/DEVIN	Ryan Spahn
KENDRA/JENNA	Jennifer Kim
ANI/SASHA/CALLIE	Catherine Combs
GLORIA/NAN	Jeanine Serralles
MILES/SHAWN/RASHAAD	Kyle Beltran
LORIN	Michael Crane

Gloria received its European premiere at Hampstead Theatre (Edward Hall, Artistic Director; Greg Ripley-Duggan, Executive Producer) in London on June 21, 2017. It was directed by Michael Longhurst. The designer was Lizzie Clachan, the lighting design was by Oliver Fenwick, and the sound design and composition were by Ben and Max Ringham. The cast was:

DEAN/DEVIN	Colin Morgan
KENDRA/JENNA	Kae Alexander
ANI/SASHA/CALLIE	Ellie Kendrick

CHARACTERS

DEAN/DEVIN, extra-late twenties, "white"

KENDRA/JENNA, mid-late twenties, "Asian"

ANI/SASHA/CALLIE, early twenties, "white"

GLORIA/NAN, extra-late thirties, "anything really"

MILES/SHAWN/RASHAAD, twenty years old, "black"

LORIN, late thirties, "unclear"

SETTING

The Midtown offices of a national magazine, circa the 2010s.

NOTE

Wigs are highly encouraged.

A forward slash (/) indicates the point at which the next speaker interrupts, or simultaneous speech if at the start of a line.

ACT ONE

A cluster of four cubicles.

An upstage cubicle hides Miles, the intern, who wears head-phones and does something menial and unseen.

Another cubicle is occupied by Ani, who is in the process of printing something and preparing for her day.

The other cubicles are empty.

Upstage of the cubicles are offices enclosed in frosted glass. Other offices may be implied downstage.

As Miles and Ani work, the "Gloria" section of Bach's Mass in B Minor plays. The rhythm of Miles and Ani's working seems to coincide with the music.

At some point, a printer somewhere starts churning, beeps, then stops. Ani notices. She tries to get Miles's attention, but can barely be heard over the music.

ANI: Miles?

(No answer.)

Miles? . . . Miles? *(Pokes her head over the divider)* Miles!

(Miles notices her, takes off his headphones, the song cuts out.)

MILES: Yep?
ANI: I think the printer is out of / paper. Could you—
MILES: Oh yeah. No problem.

(Miles gets up and exits to an offstage supply closet, leaving Ani onstage working for a bit before her phone rings. She answers.)

ANI: Good morning. Arthur Kimble's office . . . Yes, one second . . . *(Presses buttons, transferring the call)* Hey—I have Jonah on the line . . . Okay, great.

(Ani transfers the call as Dean rushes in with his man-bag, looking generally like a mess. He starts getting situated in his cubicle.)

It's 10:48.
DEAN: Shut up. I still beat Kendra.
ANI: Are you hungover?
DEAN: What do you think?
ANI: Where were you last night?
DEAN: Gloria's housewarming.
ANI: Wait—you actually went?
DEAN: I thought we all were going! Why didn't you text me back?
ANI: Oh no! I thought we were joking!
DEAN: How would me texting you "are you coming to Gloria's" even be a joke?!
ANI: I totally thought you were texting me as if you were actually at the party but you really weren't.
DEAN: Why would I ever do that, Ani!?

8

ANI: I don't know—it just seems like something you would do! I was never going to go to Gloria's. She's, like, an emotional terrorist.

DEAN: Yeah, well, once I showed up last night and realized I was the only idiot who came, I had to drink enough to forget I was there, so, for the record, the way I feel is sort of your fault!

ANI: I'm so sorry! Was it awful?

DEAN: So awful. So so so awful—and *sad*—

ANI: Oh no—

(Miles reenters with the printer paper.)

DEAN: No one showed up and she'd hired a bartender and everything— *(Seeing Miles, pulling himself up, brightly)* Good morning, Miles!

MILES: Good morning.

DEAN: I'll come by with something for you to do in just a second.

MILES: Okay, no rush.

DEAN *(Whispering to Ani, harshly)*: How early did he get here?

ANI *(Whispering)*: He was here when I got here.

DEAN *(Still whispering)*: Why would you show up before your supervisors? This is an internship. That is so weird—

ANI: Wait—*no one else* was there?

DEAN: Well no one else from Edit. Lydia from Photo was there, for like, a minute and the new guy in Copy, but they were smart enough to be on their way to another party. Unless they were lying? Oh my god they were lying!

ANI: How long did you stay?

DEAN: Until the end basically—

ANI: What? Oh no!

DEAN: I didn't know what else to do! I felt so bad. And Gloria totally knew what was happening. She basically hid in her kitchen all night, slicing limes for no reason, while the rest of us sat around making this painful small talk. It was so embarrassing—

9

ANI: Ugh. I'm so sorry. But see what she did? She held you hostage—emotionally—like a terrorist. You can't let her do that—

DEAN: I felt bad.

ANI: Yeah, well don't. We're grown-ups, which means we get to choose our friends.

DEAN (*Brightly again*): Hey, Miles?

MILES: Yeah?

DEAN: Can you come here for a second?

MILES (*Coming here*): Sure.

DEAN (*Giving him money*): Can you take this and go get a coconut water from the vending machines?

MILES: Sure . . .

(*Miles exits.*)

ANI: You are the worst.

DEAN: He's an intern.

ANI: No one ever made you get a coconut water.

DEAN: No, but it was different back then.

ANI: Five whole years ago?

DEAN: You've only been here a year, Anica, but yes: "back then" internships were real because you actually had to do this thing called "apply for it" and there were no "labor laws" "protecting" you so no one gave you a "stipend" and the work you did was real because you were basically auditioning for a job. That's how I started. That's how Sasha started before me, even Crystal before you. Now all these baby Ivy League fucks, they just waltz in here on a recommendation from their fancy professors just looking to pad their stupid résumés—and then we're stuck running some sort of summer camp—literally making up busy work for them to do on top of our actual work because they're too entitled to do anything else and they know they'll just get handed better jobs than ours right after college anyway or start their own internet media platform digital stupid space app dummy stupid thing and make a billion dollars selling it to Facebook. This kid should be getting people coconut waters for the life experience. *(Gesturing to something on her desk)* Can I borrow your—

ANI: Of course.

(Ani hands Dean a bottle of headache medicine just as Miles is returning with the coconut water.)

MILES: Here you go.

DEAN: Thanks, Miles. I'll be over in like a second.

MILES: Okay. No worries.

(Miles wanders back over to his desk, crossing paths with Kendra, who struts in with some Starbucks and a shopping bag.)

KENDRA *(To Miles, brightly)*: Morning!

MILES: Good morning.

KENDRA *(Noticing Miles at his desk)*: Oh my god look how sweet you are! Are you already hard at work? And it's not even lunchtime— You're making us all look bad!

DEAN: I think he's just making you look bad, Kendra. We all came to work on time.

KENDRA: Dean, what's going on? Why do you look like you've raped yourself?

ANI: He went to Gloria's thing last night.

KENDRA: No! You went?!

ANI: And he stayed the whole time.

KENDRA: What?! Why?!

DEAN: I thought Ani would be there.

KENDRA: I thought you guys were joking?—

ANI: See?

DEAN *(Noticing her shopping bags)*: And I'm sorry—did you actually go shopping instead of coming to work?

KENDRA: First of all, Eleanor is working from home this morning. Second of all, I have been on the clock since I got on the train because, FYI, we live in the age of smartphones and if Eleanor needs something she emails me. Third of all, I am reporting.

ANI: Reporting what?

KENDRA: I am writing a blogpost on sample-sale culture.

DEAN: For us?

KENDRA: I don't know yet. It's on spec.

DEAN: So, in other words, you just went shopping.

KENDRA: Stupid Kara gets to leave work all the time to cover some stupid street fair for trans people or some crap—

DEAN: That's because she gets actual assignments—

KENDRA: Right, because her boss is the web editor and borderline illiterate and basically out to lunch all the time. So Kara is rewarded for literally being in his visual field and gets a million bylines even though she is a terrible writer. This place is so fucked up. Your whole fate depends on who you wind up working for. If I—or any of us— had wound up the web assistant or the news assistant or Michael's assistant, we'd be much farther along in our careers right now. Instead we rot away down here in "culture" so everyone forgets about us.

ANI: I feel pretty good about where I am in my career.

KENDRA: You just got here. Give it a year. *(Showing her the blouse)* Look at this cute blouse I found!

DEAN: That's the exact blouse you're wearing right now.

KENDRA: No, Dean, you can't borrow it. *(Beat, reading something)* Wait, what is this weird email from Bo?

ANI: I know, I was just reading that.

KENDRA: They're getting rid of the coffee machine in the snack room?! First they stop reimbursing our cabs, then they freeze our raises and now we have to bring our own coffee?

ANI: Don't you already bring your own coffee?

KENDRA: Yes, but what if I need another cup?

DEAN: Then you'll leave for Starbucks in the middle of the day like you always do.

KENDRA: The point is people here are already exploited enough. You'd think they'd garnish a figure off of their ridiculous salaries before they went after our shitty free coffee. Why does it feel like we're on the freaking *Titanic?*

(A door opens and Nan, unseen, speaks. She sounds a little miffed—or a little ill—or both.)

NAN *(Offstage)*: Dean?

DEAN: Nan—just finishing something up—sorry— *(Beat, seeing her)* Are you okay?

NAN *(Offstage, a little impatient)*: I'm fine. Can we get started?

DEAN: Yeah, sorry. I'll be right there.

(Nan disappears back into her office, as Dean gets up, grabs a notepad.)

Fuck / me—

KENDRA: Nice.

ANI: What's happening?

DEAN: Nan is flying out this afternoon for the Edinburgh Book Fair and business made her book an earlier flight because it was cheaper so now I have to reschedule half the meetings before the offices over there close.

(Dean exits into Nan's office.)

KENDRA: Ani, did Dean just get here?

ANI: Yeah. Like ten minutes before you did.

KENDRA: What a douche. And also, is he going for some sort of record?

ANI: What do you mean?

KENDRA: Isn't this the third time this week he's come in hungover? *(To Miles)* Miles, see? I want you to be careful. Too much networking turns you into an alcoholic.

ANI: Kendra.

KENDRA: What? I'm imparting professional wisdom, Ani. That is our responsibility as supervisors.

ANI: It's actually just really bitchy.

KENDRA: Come on. I *love* Dean! We *all* love him—I mean, he's clearly got all this potential—he's always had it—but what has he actually done with it? Nothing. And why? Because he spends every night out chumming it up with the whole industry at every stupid networking opportunity he can find and every day recovering from the hangover and it's just a sad, vicious cycle.

ANI: Gloria's housewarming was not a networking opportunity.

KENDRA: Ani, do you know how long Gloria's been here?

ANI: I don't know.

KENDRA: Like fifteen years. Which means that not only has she sat around in Copy for over a decade losing her mind because no one here has the balls to tell people they'll never be promoted or to just, like, fire them and put them out of their misery—but Gloria's also had the good fortune of getting to know and watch, like, who knows however many generations of assistants come through here and go on to become, like, some hotshot editor or big reporter somewhere else. I'm willing to put money on the fact that Dean thought some of those people would show up and he would get to, like, starfuck until sun-up. Why do you think he actually stayed the whole time? But he obviously miscalculated. And why? Because Gloria is the office freak and no one wants to hang with the office freak outside the office, which Dean would have noticed if he wasn't so desperate and drunk and we all know heavy drinking impairs your judgment, which brings me back to my original point: "schmoozers become boozers." I just made that up. If Nan had half a brain, she would take away his expense account and put that money towards rehab. And, honestly, for the both of them. That woman's about as big of a lush as he is. The only difference is, somehow, she manages to work through the hangovers. I think I've had a lot of caffeine—

ANI: I just think Dean was being nice.

KENDRA: Yeah, okay.

ANI: And I think it's really inappropriate for you to be saying all this behind his back and in front of our intern—

KENDRA: I'm just concerned, Ani. And I will say it to his face. And I think it's better Intern hears it here than out on the street. Isn't that right, Intern?

(Beat, no answer.)

(Turns to look) Oh wait, he has his headphones on.

ANI: Good.

MILES *(Taking his headphones off)*: What?

KENDRA: Nothing. Actually, can you take this and get me a Luna Bar from the vending machines?

(Kendra gives him some money. Miles goes, just as Gloria comes stalking in. There is a purse around her shoulder, which she clutches. She stops in front of Dean's empty cubicle. Her energy is way weird.)

ANI: Speaking of: Hi, Gloria!

GLORIA: "Speaking of"?

ANI: We were just talking about you.

GLORIA: Why were you just talking about me?

ANI: Your party. I'm so sorry I couldn't make it last night. Dean said it was really nice.

GLORIA *(A little taken aback)*: He did?

ANI: Yeah. Did you have fun?

GLORIA *(Cold)*: Not really.

ANI: Oh.

(Beat, as Gloria stares at Ani intensely, perhaps clutching her purse a little tighter. Ani feels a little freaked out.)

GLORIA: Where is Dean?

ANI *(Freaked out)*: Uh, he's meeting with Nan right now.

GLORIA: Okay. I have to go.

(Gloria stalks off.)

ANI: What the fuck was that?

KENDRA: What the fuck was what?

ANI: She just like stared at me like this for like three minutes. *(Stares at Kendra like Gloria)* Like a crazy person.

KENDRA: Gloria is a crazy person.

ANI: No, this was like uncharacteristically crazy. Like bitchy.

KENDRA: You brought it on yourself.

ANI: What?

KENDRA: You think you're the first person to "apologize" for skipping her dumb party? If this woman didn't know her social standing around the office before, she certainly knows it now. I'd be a bitch, too.

ANI: Well, you didn't go to her party and she didn't say anything to you.

KENDRA: She never says anything to me. Gloria and I have an understanding that she and I have no reason to ever speak to each other ever. Unlike you and Dean, I don't believe there's a point in being fake to her.

(Miles reenters.)

ANI: I'm not being fake. I'm being polite.

MILES: Here you go.

KENDRA: Thank you, Miles.

(Beat, in which everyone "works." Ani's phone rings.)

ANI: Arthur Kimble's office.

(Beat.)

Hi, Clara. He's meeting with a writer at the moment, but can he call you right back?

(Beat.)

Okay great.

(Ani hangs up the phone.)

KENDRA: Oh my god, Sarah Tweed is dead?!
ANI: What?
KENDRA: They found her body this morning! Oh my god. An overdose?
ANI: How am I just hearing about this?!
MILES: Who is Sarah Tweed?
KENDRA: Oh my god are you kidding me? / Ani—
ANI: This is so sad. What?
KENDRA: Miles just asked me who Sarah Tweed is.
ANI: What?
KENDRA: Now I feel a hundred years old.
MILES: So who is she?
ANI: I'll find you one of her songs.
KENDRA: Oh my god I used to love Sarah Tweed.

(A moody song begins playing from Ani's computer. Ani awkwardly sings along for a bar or two like a girl who thinks she likes to sing but really doesn't.)

MILES: I have never heard this before.
KENDRA: Is this from *Ophelia Street*?
ANI: No. It's from *Glitter Witch*.
KENDRA: Duh—
ANI: I was obsessed with this album for an entire year of my life.
KENDRA: She got me through such a bad depression.

(Beat.)

Oh my god, wait, this is my favorite part!

ANI: Me, too!

(Ani and Kendra half-sing that part of the song together.)

MILES: You guys are so weird.

KENDRA: You're weird.

(Dean finally emerges from Nan's office.)

DEAN *(Into Nan's office)*: Okay, well, let me know if you need me / to get you anything, aspirin or . . .

KENDRA: I love this song.

(Dean goes to his desk and grabs some manuscripts.)

ANI: What's wrong with Nan?

DEAN: She's sick.

KENDRA: You mean hungover? Are you guys like how dogs start to resemble their owners?

(Dean flips Kendra off.)

DEAN: Ew. Is this Sarah Tweed? Why are we playing this?

KENDRA: In memoriam.

DEAN: What?

ANI: / She died.

KENDRA: / She died.

DEAN: What? When?

KENDRA: Last night.

DEAN: OD?

KENDRA: Yes.

DEAN: OMG— Called it.

ANI: Rude. I loved her.

KENDRA: Is this song really ten years old?

ANI: Oh my god what? Where has my life gone?

DEAN: Oh, Ani, shut up—

KENDRA: Yeah, aren't you, like, twenty-four?

DEAN *(Dropping manuscripts off with Miles)*: Okay, Miles, it's your lucky day. I've got to reschedule a bunch of meetings this morning, so you get to do first pass on some books for excerpt. So: read these and get me evals by the end of the day, okay?

MILES: Yeah, sure.

DEAN: And, uh, take your time. Don't work so hard. We're not paying you enough. And don't feel like you have to show up at nine A.M.

MILES *(With a laugh)*: Okay, I'll remember that for tomorrow.

(Miles puts on some headphones, starts sorting through the book manuscripts.)

DEAN *(Beat, crossing back to his desk)*: This song is so terrible.

KENDRA: You're terrible. *(Remembering)* Oh shit. Is it Thursday?

DEAN: Yes.

(Kendra picks up a phone and dials a number. She waits for someone to pick up and motions for Ani to turn the music down a bit. Ani complies. Meanwhile, everyone else starts to "work." Kendra proceeds to have a long discussion in Chinese or Korean—whichever the actress can speak/fake.)

KENDRA *(In another language)*: Hey, Dad. Is Mom there? . . . Can I speak to her? Okay . . .

DEAN *(To Ani)*: Is Kendra serious right now?

ANI: I know. I can't.

KENDRA *(Still into the phone, still in another language)*: Mom— Hi! I totally forgot it was your birthday! / I meant to call yesterday but I was so busy— Happy Birthday! . . . I can't talk long, because I'm at work, but how are you feeling?

Good! Are you healing okay? Are the pills helping? The radiation? Good . . . Good . . . Okay . . . Well I have to go. I'm at work. Okay. I love you! Bye!

(Beat. They work.)

ANI: Oh, Dean, Gloria came by looking for you earlier.
DEAN: Why?
ANI: I have no idea. But she was in like extra-crazy mode.
MILES *(Taking out his headphones)*: Hey, Dean?
DEAN: Yes, Miles?
MILES *(Holding out something for him)*: I think you accidentally left this in the pile.
DEAN *(Snatching it away, kind of freaking out)*: / Oh my god! Thank you.
ANI: What is that?
DEAN: Nothing. Thank you, Miles.
MILES: No problem.

(Miles goes back to his reading.)

ANI *(To Dean)*: What is that?
DEAN: / Nothing.
ANI: Then why did you freak out like that? Let me see!
DEAN: No.
ANI: What was it, Miles?
DEAN *(Snapping)*: Stop, Ani! Mind your business!
KENDRA *(Hanging up)*: You guys—what the hell! I was on the phone!
DEAN: You were on a personal call—

(Lorin—a sad sad sad sad guy—sort of stalks in, goes over to Ani's cubicle.)

LORIN: Hey, I'm sorry, you guys, but— *(Distracted, to Ani)* Can you—can you please turn that off? Please?—
ANI *(Turning it off)*: Sorry, sorry, sorry—

LORIN *(To everyone)*: We are all trying to work down the hall, so if you could just please please just keep it down a little bit, we'd really appreciate it? I know it seems like you're isolated, but this hallway / actually carries sound—

KENDRA: Carries sound— / we know—

LORIN: And we can basically hear everything, so please. Thanks.

KENDRA: We'll keep it down.

(Lorin leaves.)

DEAN: Oh my god, Lorin, eat a dick.

ANI: Be nice! Fact-checking is hard.

DEAN: The issue is closed. He's just being annoying—like he's the only person ever doing any work. Get headphones like everyone else.

KENDRA: It's gotten worse since he's been promoted.

ANI: Maybe he's under more stress?

KENDRA: Okay, we get it, Ani. You're in love with him.

ANI: / Kendra!

DEAN: What?

KENDRA: What? The way you flirt—it's so obvious. Besides, this office could use another couple besides Lucy and Marcus. / Yuck.

DEAN: Since when do you have a crush on Lorin?

ANI: I do not have a crush on Lorin—oh my god.

KENDRA: That's not how you were acting at the last office party. Though did we ever find out if he's gay?

DEAN: Lorin is not *gay*.

KENDRA: How do you know?

DEAN: We all know each other. I mean, I think he might be *Jewish?*

ANI: No, his mom is Mexican—

KENDRA: You guys, Lorin is a harried, passive-aggressive shell of himself and that has nothing to do with *race*. It's just what happens when you stay in this hideous place for too long. It could happen to any of us.

DEAN: Really, Kendra? The intern is right there.

KENDRA: He has his headphones in. And, Ani, I hope you're paying attention. I know your whole thing is like, "Oh, I'm so pretty. I'm a pretty nerd, who graduated from college a year early with like a neuroscience degree and was going to go to clone like baby brains but accidentally wound up in magazines because I know computer stuff but if it doesn't work out I can always just go to like brain school or computer school or wherever pretty nerds go."

(Beat.)

But you better start figuring your shit out. Get a five-year plan. Because if you don't, you're going to wake up one day and the thing you thought would be an interesting thing to do after college is actually your career and then you have to live with it.

(Dean burps loudly.)

Ew. For example: this cautionary tale.

DEAN: Excuse me?

KENDRA: Don't you hold the title for Longest Living Assistant on Edit Row?

DEAN: Daisy's been here the longest.

KENDRA: Daisy doesn't count. She's the assistant to the editor-in-chief, which is basically an associate editor. And I said "longest living." Aren't *you* turning thirty any day now? I will die before I turn thirty in a cubicle.

DEAN: Really? Tell me how to help you get there?

(Beat.)

And Daisy is not a fucking associate editor. First of all, she just ghost-edits all the writers Michael doesn't want. Second of all, if you're in a cubicle, you're an assistant.

KENDRA: Okay, Dean. Believe what you need to believe.

ANI: What's your five-year plan, Kendra?

KENDRA: What do you mean?

ANI: You're twenty-seven. That gives you only three years.

KENDRA: Um I am clearly making healthy strides towards an exit.

DEAN: With what? Your fifteen fake Twitter accounts or your Instagram full of dresses?

KENDRA: Eat me. At least I'm getting my name out there. I guess I should be on the Drunk Uncle Dean plan, getting wasted every night and continue waiting around here for a promotion that's never going to happen?

DEAN: Kendra, do some work.

KENDRA: If you had half a brain, you'd look around and see everyone in charge is pushing sixty, or just past it and they're not going anywhere and they are certainly not thinking about you. These post-war glutton-babies were spoiled on the riches of being an American when being an American was basically the Best and also, by freak chance, just happened to discover New York when it, too, was also the Best and apartments were like a dollar. And now, all these decades later, here we are. Now that the publishing world's collapsed and contracting all around us, mainly because they were too busy bluffing and boozing their way through the eighties-slash-nineties, as opposed to, I don't know, anticipating the internet—now that all the martini lunches have all dried up, all these boomers are like, "Wait, I think being a good editor and building a sustainable media industry is actually a skill that requires work. What is this work? How do you do it? Can I do it now?" And suddenly realizing how disposable they've made themselves. In the meantime, who has historically been doing all the work? The poor suckers born a generation later. It's the assistants. Like us—some of us who think they're going to rise through the ranks like their bosses did without realizing that these editors were all assistants, again, by freak chance, in the exact historical window when this city actually had a fuck-ton of opportunity in it and not just the illusion of it. And do you know why? Because people actually died back then. There was something called *turnover*. Now these boomers aren't dying. And they know it. And, if we're not careful, they're going to starve us / out—

(Nan is heard vomiting loudly through the office door, cutting everyone off. Beat.)

NAN *(Offstage)*: Dean?

(Dean goes to Nan's door.)

ANI *(To Kendra)*: Did she just throw up?
DEAN: Nan? Are you okay?
NAN *(Offstage)*: I'm fine.
DEAN: Are you sure?
NAN *(Offstage)*: Yes. But can you come here for a second?
KENDRA *(To Ani)*: See what I mean? Dog and owner.

(Once Dean has exited, Ani gets up and goes around to look at the document on Dean's desk, nosily.)

ANI: Kendra.
KENDRA: What?
ANI: Dean has a book proposal on his desk.
KENDRA: So?
ANI: It's his.
KENDRA *(Getting up to go see)*: He does not!
ANI: A memoir.
KENDRA: About what?
ANI: *'Zine Dreams, or Ambition.* "*'Zine Dreams*"? "*'Zine*"? *(Gasps)* Is that supposed to be short for "magazines"?

KENDRA: Oh god. "New York City is a rat race and this is the story of one young professional's laps in it. This is about climbing every ladder of a publishing world only to find yourself stuck in the same pit." What does that even mean?

(Nan's door opens and Dean backs out of it, holding something. Ani and Kendra run to their desks, guiltily, but Dean doesn't notice.)

DEAN *(To Nan)*: Are you sure you can get on the plane?
NAN *(Offstage)*: I'm sure. Please. I just have to get back to work.
DEAN: Okay.
NAN: Thank you, Dean.
DEAN: No problem.

(Dean closes the door.)

ANI *(Back at her cubicle)*: What happened?

(Dean turns around slowly. He is holding a plastic bag full of vomit.)

KENDRA: Dean, please tell me that is not what I think it is!

(Silently, sadly, but swiftly, as if he, too, might upchuck, Dean runs offstage.)

ANI: Oh my god ew. Is that bag full of puke?
MILES *(Taking his headphones off)*: What's going on?
KENDRA: Dean just walked out of Nan's office holding a bag of puke.
MILES *(Peeking around the cubicle)*: Ew. What?

(Dean returns shamefully, looking blanched.)

ANI: Are you okay?

DEAN: I don't want to talk about it.

KENDRA: I'm sure that helped your hangover.

ANI: Wait, are you going to throw up, too? Because I have a thing with throw-up.

DEAN: I don't know.

ANI: I could get you a ginger ale or something?

DEAN: I think I just need some caffeine.

KENDRA: What caffeine? There's no more coffee in the snack room. But I'm probably going to make a Starbucks run in a bit, if you want something.

(Kendra drains the dregs of her Starbucks.)

DEAN: Kendra, how do you get away with this?

KENDRA: Get away with what?

DEAN: Doing no work. You just got here an hour late, called China or something, monologued about baby boomers for fifteen minutes, and now you're leaving on a coffee break? Does Eleanor just literally have nothing for you to do?

KENDRA: It's not my fault my boss is self-sufficient enough to clean up her own puke. Eleanor, as a woman who has managed to make a name for herself in this shitty industry still dominated by privileged straight white men, is sensitive to the demands on my time—

DEAN: Kendra, you're a rich Asian girl from Pasadena with a degree from Harvard. That is essentially a privileged straight white man.

KENDRA: How privileged and white and male of you to say. And also, somehow, very gay. I can't wait to read about it in *'Zine Dreams.*

(Beat, as Dean realizes.)

DEAN: Fuck you guys! You went through my desk?!

KENDRA: Ani went through it.

DEAN: Ani!

KENDRA: Here I was thinking you were wasting away on the editor track. See, Ani? Even Dean had an escape plan. I have to admit I'm kind of impressed. You're not as dumb as you act. Just don't open the book with your stupid monastery story.

ANI: What monastery story?

DEAN: Kendra, please shut up. Some of us are trying to work.

KENDRA: Wait, did you not know that Dean tried to be a Buddhist monk? It's like the only interesting thing about him, and it's not even that interesting—

DEAN: Kendra, will you shut up? Will you shut the fuck up before I fucking kill you?

KENDRA: Um, should I contact HR?

DEAN: Do I need to rip off your big fucking ugly mouth and piss down your / fucking throat in order to get you and your stupid fucking face to shut the fuck up!

ANI: You guys . . . you guys . . . you guys . . . you guys . . . you guys—

(Lorin reenters.)

LORIN: I'm sorry but really, guys? Really? I'm really really not trying to be annoying, but can you guys please please please keep it down? Please, okay? I am asking you so nicely. We are working on a really insane deadline.

DEAN: Lorin, what is happening?

LORIN: We're running this last-minute feature on some singer named Sarah Tweed—

DEAN: / What?

ANI: / What?

KENDRA: / Wait, what?!

LORIN: She died.

KENDRA: We know. How are they featuring her now?

LORIN: Yeah, weirdly enough we've had this blog post that Kara wrote in inventory, that's randomly becoming timely, so they want to beef it up into a profile and we're rushing it into the next issue.

ANI: / What? Why?

KENDRA: Are you kidding?

LORIN: I know. It's fucking retarded. I'm sitting here waiting to be called back by some twenty-six year old who happens to be the one person in the world with a PhD on Sarah Tweed. I'm thirty-seven and all I have is a BA in French. Like why did I do that? I'm not French! My family's not French! I was supposed to be a lawyer. Someone shoot me.

(Lorin exits.)

KENDRA: This is so unfair! Why is Kara getting to write about Sarah Tweed?!

DEAN: It sounds like she already wrote about her.

KENDRA: It was a blog post! It was filler for their dumb website! You know that means she only tossed it off in like forty-five minutes and now it's being rushed into the next issue? Why does it always happen like this? This girl didn't write a single thing before she got here!

ANI: It's actually pretty good . . .

KENDRA: What?

ANI: She already filed a draft. It's in the system.

KENDRA *(Frantically searching her computer)*: What?! *(Beat, as she reads the piece on her computer)* Wha . . . Are you . . . I . . . Oh my fucking god. And what the fuck is this title? "Serenading Sappho"? Why is Kara trying to make Sarah Tweed look like some huge lesbian!

DEAN: Wasn't she?

KENDRA: She dated like three girls! She was bi! Kara's just got some weird lesbian agenda where she's trying to make this a gay suicide or something. Should I say something to her? I'm going to say something.

DEAN: You'd have to say something to the editor.

KENDRA: You're right! Who's the editor?

DEAN: Austin.

KENDRA: Jesus Christ. Of course it's fucking Austin. I'm totally going to do it. I'll just walk up to Austin and be like, "Hey, I read Kara's piece. I'm a huge Sarah Tweed fan, I just read the draft and I just noticed some things." Ani, come with me!

ANI: Leave me out of it.

KENDRA: You are such a pussy! This is a conspiracy! We are the actual Cultural Department and just as qualified as the other end of that hallway and no one remembers us and then we have to stand by and watch this artist we love— this artist we cherish—get written about poorly the day after she dies? We have to take a stand against this! We have to like remind people that we're here, you guys! I'm gonna do it!

DEAN: Do it!

KENDRA: I'm doing it!

(Kendra stands up, resolutely walks off.)

ANI: Where does it say that Austin is editing the piece?

DEAN: Nowhere. I just made that up to get her the fuck away from me.

ANI: Oh my god! That was so mean, Dean! What did you just do?

DEAN: So I could get some work done. *(A lesson)* Don't go through my desk. *(Noticing Ani exiting)* Where are you going?

ANI: I clearly need to go watch this?

(Ani scurries off after Kendra. Dean and Miles remain, sort of working. Gloria comes stalking around the corner, sees Dean.)

GLORIA: Hey.

DEAN: Hey, Gloria. Ani said you were looking for me earlier, what's up?

GLORIA: Uh, nothing. I figured it out.

DEAN: Okay . . . Can I help you with something?

GLORIA: Where did Ani and Kendra go?

DEAN: Ani's watching Kendra confront Austin about something Kara wrote. Do you need them?

GLORIA: No.

DEAN: Okay.

(Beat.)

How are you?

GLORIA: Fine.

DEAN: Last night was fun!

(Gloria stares at him for a long time, like she's about to say something, hands trembling in her pockets. Then, suddenly, she just stalks off, leaving Dean behind, completely weirded out.)

MILES: Was that Gloria?

DEAN: Yes.

MILES: Yikes.

DEAN: I know. She's a little weird.

MILES: Yeah—I heard you guys talking about her just now.

DEAN: I thought your headphones were on?

MILES: Yeah but I haven't really been listening to anything for a while.

(Beat.)

Hey, Dean.

DEAN: Yes?

MILES: I only glanced at the cover letter, but I thought your book sounded good. I'd totally read it.

DEAN: Thanks.

MILES: Yeah, I had no idea you were a Buddhist.

DEAN: I'm not a Buddhist. I worked in a monastery. And it was only, like, a few months. It was bullshit.

MILES: Then why did you do it?

DEAN: I was dating someone in college who was really into Buddhism and it was this person's idea to basically try and live there and work there and I thought it would be interesting and worth writing about, but then I realized that Buddhist monasteries are just boring as shit and they work the volunteers like slaves. And this person I was dating turned out to be a total psycho. So I just left. And I moved to New York.

MILES: Ah.

(Beat.)

Maybe I should write a book.

DEAN: Uh, do you have something to write about?

MILES: Not yet, but I mean I feel like I could figure it out. Did you have something to write about before you decided to be a writer?

DEAN: Not exactly.

MILES: Well then how did you know that you were a writer?

DEAN: I've just always felt it. Since I was young. But it took me a while to start writing anything good. I needed some experience.

MILES: I admire people who've always known what they wanted to do. I've like never known.

DEAN: I bet you're just naturally good at everything, huh?

MILES *(With a laugh)*: No—I can't even figure out what I'm going to do after college. I was actually thinking about grad school or J school or something but now I think I want to wait maybe. I don't even know if I want to be a writer or an editor or work in magazines, really. My professor just thought I would be good at it.

DEAN: Yeah, Richard loves you—

MILES: Do you like working in magazines? Well, obviously not, since you're writing a book—

DEAN: That's not true. I'm just ready for a change.

MILES: Yeah. Yeah, me, too. I only just realized that I've spent my entire life in school. I think I might need to experience the real world. I'm actually thinking about maybe going abroad and just like teaching English. Just somewhere like really far away and random. Like Germany or Japan or something, but I'm really interested in Africa, though. Did you know that, within our lifetime, they're expecting like two-thirds of the population of the whole continent to just be like . . . gone? Just totally wiped out. I suddenly feel this deep anxiety about the future, about how everything I know now could just be gone one day— or like everything on the Earth right now at this exact moment could be totally different tomorrow.

DEAN: Yeah. Listen, I've got to get back to rescheduling these meetings.

MILES: Oh, oh yeah, I'm sorry.

(Beat before Miles goes back to his cubicle.)

So Nan's going to be gone tomorrow?

DEAN: Yeah. She's flying out this afternoon for a book fair in Scotland.

MILES: When is she leaving?

DEAN: Well, she's about to leave for a noon lunch, and then I don't really know if she'll be back to the office before she heads to the airport.

MILES: Oh. Then do you think she'll have like a second to speak to me before she leaves? Just like a second.

DEAN: I don't know.

MILES: 'Cause, you know, tomorrow is my last day—

DEAN: No it isn't?

MILES: Yeah, it is. It's been eight weeks.

DEAN: Holy crap. I didn't even realize—

MILES: Ha ha ha. Yeah, time flies. I just feel like I just want to say a proper goodbye before she left. Just you know, to say goodbye. Just really quick. Is she going to have time?

DEAN: I mean, I don't know. She's also a little sick.

MILES: Do you think that you could ask her?

DEAN: Um. Sure. *(Picks up the phone and dials)* Nan? The intern's last day is tomorrow and he's wondering if he can come say goodbye before you— Are you going to have time? I told him you— Yes . . . It's Miles. Okay. *(Hangs up)* She said you can pop your head in right now if you want.

MILES: Cool.

DEAN: Just knock.

(Miles gets up, goes to the door, knocks.)

MILES: Hey, Nan?

NAN *(Offstage)*: Miles! Come in, come in—

MILES: I just want—

NAN *(Offstage)*: Come in. You can close the door.

MILES: Wha—okay.

(Miles closes the door. Dean looks a little alarmed, just as Ani is seen scurrying back, past Miles, making her way to her desk.)

ANI: Shit shit shit shit shit—

DEAN: What happened?

(Kendra stalks back in, looking really unhappy.)

KENDRA: You are a fucking asshole!

DEAN: What happened?

KENDRA: Austin is not editing Kara's piece, you shit!

DEAN: Really? Who is?

KENDRA: Eleanor is, you piece of shit!

DEAN: You don't know what your own boss is editing?

KENDRA: Eleanor is working from home!

DEAN: Wow, so you really do have nothing to do.

KENDRA: You set me up! That is not cool! I would never do that to you!

DEAN: I had no idea about Eleanor. I swear.

KENDRA: And now because of you Michael thinks I'm an idiot!

DEAN: Michael?

KENDRA: Yes! Because, after Austin told me he wasn't editing the print piece and I realized you were a fucking liar, that asshole, like, calls Kara in and is, like, "Why don't you give her your notes yourself," and so, like, in stalks Kara, who I guess had been eavesdropping and she's like, "What notes?" And I had no choice but to just bring up some of the liberties she took with Sarah Tweed's sexuality and, I guess, this strikes a nerve with her because she's so insecure and knows she's not supposed to be writing this, so she starts screaming at me, accusing me of being homophobic, which is not fair because I totally have a gay brother—I think—and then Michael comes over from next door and he's like, "What is going on?" And Austin's all, "Kendra is just giving Kara some notes on the Sarah Tweed piece," with this shit-eating grin on his face. Then Michael's like, "Are these coming from Eleanor?" And I'm just like, "No, they're coming from me, why?" And then Michael's like, "Because I just assigned the piece to Eleanor, like an hour ago and if you have any notes you should be giving them to her . . . your boss." And then the room gets really quiet and I have to make up some excuse about how Eleanor's been in meetings all morning, so I haven't been, and I look like a fucking asshole when you and Kara are the fucking assholes!

ANI: How is this Kara's fault?

KENDRA: Because she turned a very professional conversation into some sort of catfight and tried to imply I was there to sabotage her—

DEAN: Which you were—

KENDRA: No I was not! I was trying to help!

DEAN: Kendra, you know, Kara's in the middle of closing a piece that's turning around in a day.

KENDRA: So? It's been in inventory for months. It was basically dead—

DEAN: Still she has to fluff it up to a profile in a day. I know this may sound a little foreign to you since you spent half your day in line for sample sales, but when people actually do work, it's actually stressful and you're sort of tired and the last thing you want is someone trying to "help you" by fucking with it.

KENDRA: Thanks for the life lesson. Now I have to warn Eleanor about this shit show— You know what, you people are fucking losers who can go fuck yourselves. Except for you, Miles. Wait, where is Miles?

DEAN: Saying goodbye to Nan.

KENDRA: Oh good. I hope he's interviewing for your job.

DEAN: Ha ha.

KENDRA: Or maybe he's telling her about your book proposal.

DEAN: Oh, shut up.

KENDRA: Or maybe he's telling her about your book and interviewing for your job at the same time. You know, Nan has seemed unimpressed with you lately. And Miles is young and smart and capable and not a drunk—

DEAN: Why don't you tweet about it on one of your Twitters?

KENDRA: *Zine Dreams*. What makes you think anything about your miserable little life is worth reading about?

DEAN: / Tweet tweet—

KENDRA: The last thing the world needs is another memoir of a drunk white guy wasting away his twenties in New York—I'M GOING TO STARBUCKS!

(Kendra grabs her purse and leaves. Lorin comes over.)

LORIN: Are you people kidding me?

DEAN: Do you need to borrow a pair of headphones?

LORIN: I have my own headphones and I can still hear you! Over my sixty-dollar-noise-canceling headphones, I can still hear you, because what you are making is more than noise, okay?! You're like a kindergarten over here!

DEAN: Sorry.

ANI: How is the profile coming along?

LORIN: It looks like we're over the hard part.

DEAN: Well don't take your morning nap just yet. Kendra just psyched Kara out with a bunch of notes that she's probably going to get Eleanor to make her incorporate—

LORIN: WHAT?! ARE YOU KIDDING ME?!

DEAN: I wish. Ask Ani.

LORIN: Where did she go? I'm going to kick her in the throat!

DEAN: Starbucks.

LORIN: WHAT?!?

(Lorin suddenly starts sobbing softly. Beat, as he cries.)

ANI *(Getting up, going over to comfort him)*: Lorin?

DEAN: Are you okay?

LORIN: I'm sorry. I'm sorry. I'm just tired.

ANI: You've been up all night.

LORIN: No. Not just that. I'm fucking tired of this job. I just turned thirty-seven, you guys, and I'm still a fact-checker.

ANI: But you just got promoted—

DEAN: Yeah— You're the head fact-checker.

LORIN: That is still a fact-checker! In fact, it's worse because you're the fucking mother of all fact-checkers. You have to stay here the whole fucking night fact-checking the fact-checkers and after like six hours of fact-checking fact-checkers fact-checking all these sloppy fucking writers' facts, you just want to claw your eyes off and bleed out through your skull holes! You're just like, "What does it even matter if this is true or not? No one reads magazines for the truth! People just want something to read on the elliptical at the gym or to line their fucking canary cages with!" I don't fucking know! And it will all wind up in the trash by Friday. And then there's a fresh load of this bullshit waiting for you in your mailbox next week! And what is a "profile" actually doing besides throwing one human being after another to the wolves of history, rendering entire lives flat and uncomplicated and eight thousand words long? Like this fucking Sarah Tweed girl. Why the fuck are we only interested in her now, now that she's dead? Why does dying suddenly make someone more interesting? What the fuck is she going to do with a profile now? Sell her CDs? She's fucking dead. What is this going to do except make money for people other than her? It's so fucking fucked up. And I really envy her, you know. I wish I was dead, full of opiates in the back of a station wagon right now. I fucking wish. Anything but this bullshit! I bet she was fucking smiling when she swallowed that bottle of painkillers and climbed into that sleeping bag. I bet she was just like, "Finally, I'm getting the fuck out of this miserable existence, off of this miserable planet of people who seem like they're interested in you, but really only want you dead, who only want you when you are dead!" What is this terrible place? Why are we like this? Is another human life anything to us but an excuse to think about ourselves? Sorry, her music—I think her music is really getting to me.

ANI: What have you been listening to?

LORIN: *The Styrofoam Diary.* Ugh—everyone just suddenly feels so cruel!

DEAN: You're just having a moment.

LORIN: And did you hear about poor Gloria?

ANI: What about Gloria?

LORIN: No one went to her party last night.

ANI: Dean went.

LORIN: Oh, you did?

DEAN: I did.

LORIN: Did anyone else show up? Lydia said she went, but she left because it was so awkward.

DEAN: Yeah, there was like four people the whole night. She had all this catered food and a bartender. I got so drunk.

ANI: She actually came by here earlier and I asked her about the party and she told me she had an awful time.

LORIN: Ugh. I feel so bad. I wrote her an email. If I hadn't been here all night, I would have gone.

ANI: Really?

LORIN: Yes. Gloria's been here so long. They work her to the bone. And Copy stays later than anyone else I know, except me. This place is her life—these are, like, the people she knows. She was just finally able to scrape enough of her crap salary together to buy her own place. This is probably the hugest thing that's ever happened to her. So she pours all of her effort into throwing this party and inviting everyone and no one—*no one* could be bothered to show up? And Gloria is, okay, a little weird, but she hasn't always been this way. She's just this lady from Florida who'd been reading the magazine since she was a little girl. See? You gotta be careful, Ani: this place just turns you into a— It just sucks your soul out of you and leaves you with a fucking empty apartment. Dicks for co-workers. Your youth gone. Your friends gone. Your dreams gone. Dean knows what I'm talking about. It's good you went, man.

(Beat.)

Anyway, I have to get back to my desk, since I now know we're expecting a total rewrite. What the shit. Tell Kendra when she gets back to come see me. I'm going to smash her face in!

(Lorin exits. Beat, before the sound of laughter comes from Nan's office. Dean looks at the door.)

DEAN: What the hell?

ANI: Sounds like a fun interview. *(Off Dean's look)* Kidding.

DEAN: Not funny.

(Beat.)

You know, he just sat here and gave me this whole spiel about how he didn't know what he wanted to do after college or if he was even interested in magazines and now he's probably going down on her in there. Do you think he's after my job?

ANI: No! I just think he's just a sweet, likable guy.

DEAN: Oh please. He's just as ambitious as you or me. I promise.

ANI: I don't know if I consider myself an ambitious person.

DEAN: What?

ANI: Yeah. I like to think I'm sort of just here to see what happens.

DEAN: Yeah, because you've got actual marketable skills—

ANI: What are you talking about?

DEAN: You can do math! You know what "code" is. All I know how to do is read in one language! I don't even know what engineering is. You could go someplace else. But here's what happens to the rest of us, Ani. You wake up one day and the thing that you thought was just going to be a fun thing to do after college turns into your career—your life. And then you just have to live with that.

(Gloria comes whipping around the corner, hands in her pockets.)

GLORIA: Where did Kendra go?!

DEAN: Oh shit, she was here, but then she went to Starbucks. Do you need something?

GLORIA: Are you kidding me?! How long ago?

DEAN: I don't know. A while ago.

GLORIA: Well when is she usually back?

DEAN: It's Kendra. For all we know she's already home getting ready for bed.

GLORIA: Damnit!

ANI: Is everything okay, Gloria?

GLORIA: Yeah. It's fine! It's just you Edit people are just never at your desks! Do you guys just have like nothing to do?!

DEAN: Ha ha ha sort—

GLORIA: Fuck this!

(Gloria stalks off, hands in her pockets.)

DEAN: Um . . .

ANI: See? Extra-crazy.

(Nan's office door opens and Miles enters.)

MILES: Ha ha ha ha yes—

NAN *(Offstage, sounding much better)*: Well, have a good senior year!

MILES: Yes, thank you! Have a safe trip! And feel better!

NAN *(Offstage)*: Thanks. I will. Can you close the door?

MILES: Sure.

(Miles closes the door.)

DEAN: That was quite a goodbye.

MILES: Ha ha ha. I know. Nan is really amazing.

DEAN: She is. What were you guys laughing about?

MILES: Oh, just like . . . Professor Morrison.

DEAN: What about Rick?

MILES: Just like this funny story about him.

DEAN: Okay. And what else?

MILES: And, I don't know, she asked me what I was going to do after graduation. And I said I didn't really know and she gave me some advice.

DEAN: That's nice. What kind of advice?

MILES: Just like . . . whatever. Like general advice. Nothing specific, but she did say that I could call her if I was ever interested in working in publishing or something.

DEAN: Yeah, well, she sort of says that to everybody.

MILES: Yeah, but I don't know if I'm really interested in magazines. I mean, it seems like you guys have it pretty hard. Everyone here's so miserable, but anything you ever read about anything exciting to do or anywhere exciting to be, people aren't miserable. They're excited, you know?—

(Screaming is heard.)

DEAN: What the hell?

MILES: What is—?

(More screaming is heard.)

DEAN: It's coming from Fact-Checking. Miles, go tell *them* to shut the fuck up.

(A gunshot is heard. Maybe a few.)

MILES: Whoa—

(Miles sees what it is, goes wide-eyed.)

DEAN: What was that?

(Miles turns around and attempts to run off, past Dean and Ani. Meanwhile, the screaming grows and grows.)

ANI: Dean?

DEAN: Miles?

(Miles is just past them, when a shot is heard. Miles is hit in the back. He goes down. Dean see this. Ani sees Dean see this.)

ANI: Miles?

(A spot of blood begins to grow on Miles's back just as Gloria rushes in with a gun. She cuts behind the cubicles, coming up behind Dean and Ani.)

GLORIA: Ani.

(Ani turns around, startled, sees Gloria with the gun. Gloria shoots Ani in the face. Ani goes down behind the cubicle divider and struggles, audibly, to breathe. Gloria goes over to her and shoots her again. Silence. Dean is frozen. Gloria turns to look at him.)

DEAN: Gloria, no. No! No!

(Gloria comes around to Dean, backs him into some file cabinets. His eyes are closed. His hands are up. He's shaking. He's basically crying without tears, scared out of his mind. He wets himself.)

Please, no, no, no—please!
GLORIA: Dean.
DEAN: I'm sorry—
GLORIA: Dean.
DEAN: I'm sorry—I'm sorry—
GLORIA: I'm not going to shoot you.
DEAN *(Hears her, stops mumbling, opens eyes)*: What?
GLORIA: You were always so nice to me. Thanks.

(Beat.)

And thanks for coming to my party. You didn't have to say you had a fun time, but you did. Thanks.

(Gloria goes into a corner and raises the gun to her own head.)

DEAN: Wh—wh—wh—

(Gloria pulls the trigger. Blood splatters everywhere as—
Blackout.
In the dark, Bach's Mass in B Minor *picks up where it left off. It plays on through the intermission.)*

END OF ACT ONE

ACT TWO

Scene One

Eight months later.

A basically empty Starbucks in way West Midtown, sometime in the afternoon.

Outside, it is winter.

A bearded Dean sits at a table, reading and marking up a manuscript, cup of coffee in front of him. He listens to music on his smartphone. He doesn't look so well—a little skinnier, gaunt. His legs shake nervously. He occasionally glances out a window. He is waiting for someone.

Bach's Mass in B Minor *is still playing.*

A Starbucks employee, Shawn—who looks a lot like Miles— stands behind the counter, sort of staring at Dean. Dean catches him staring but goes back to work. Eventually, Shawn just goes for it:

SHAWN: Hey yo . . . Hey! Hey!

(He gets Dean's attention. Dean takes out his headphones and the music cuts out.)

Sorry—you just look so familiar. Do we know each other?

DEAN: I don't think so.

SHAWN: You not on TV or nothing is you?

DEAN: No.

SHAWN: A'ight. My bad. Maybe you just have one of them faces. You know, where you look like somebody? You ever get that?

DEAN: Not really.

SHAWN: There this girl who works here—Vanessa? She one of them girls that has Witherspoon face. You know how some white girls just randomly be looking like Reese Witherspoon? Vanessa be getting so mad when I say that though. She be like, "Shawn, that is racist! All white people do not look alike!" And I'm like, "Bitch, it's not racist if I say you look famous. I mean, it's only racist if I say you look like some basic run-of-the-mill white chick," you know? There's a difference. I mean people be mistaking me for somebody else all the time. And that's the shit that be getting me mad, you know? That's when I'm like, "All black people do not look alike," you know what I mean? It's like, "No, I'm not the guy who mowed your dad's lawn." And, "No, I'm not your student from the year you did Teach for America!" That's different. Vanessa just be so sensitive. It's not like I mistook her for Reese Witherspoon. It's not like I tapped her on the shoulder and was like, "Reese Witherspoon, is that you?" I just said she look *like* Reese Witherspoon, because she got a Witherspoon face. I mean, it would be different if somebody mistook me for somebody famous once in a while. That would be nice. But that, like, never happens.

(Eventually, a bundled-up Kendra has crossed past the window and enters now, maybe stomps the wet off her boots,

pulls off her hoodie. Seeing her, Dean slips his manuscript under his seat and stands to greet her.)

KENDRA: Dean, I'm so sorry I'm late—the trains / were—!
DEAN: It's okay. Totally okay. Thanks for meeting me all the way up here.
KENDRA: Of course.

(Beat.)

It's so good to see you.
DEAN: It's good to see you, too.

(Beat, as they disengage.)

How have you been?
KENDRA: I've been . . . pretty good. You know.

(Beat, as Dean looks her over.)

And how are you?
DEAN: I've been worse.
KENDRA: Right. Though, you look really good! I like the beard.
DEAN: Thanks.

(Beat.)

This is a little surreal—
KENDRA: Yeah, eight months.

(Beat.)

You know, I actually tried to get in touch, but—
DEAN: Yeah, I sort of fell / off the map—
KENDRA: And I didn't see you at anyone's funeral.

DEAN: I know, I know. I didn't—I didn't feel great about that—
but I heard they were nice.

KENDRA: They were. Especially Ani's . . . And Kara's, actually.

(Beat.)

Anyway, I'm glad you reached out.

DEAN: Can I get you something? Some kind of almond-milk
something-something?

KENDRA: Oh, no. No. I actually don't drink caffeine anymore—

DEAN: Really?

KENDRA: Yeah—I can barely set foot inside a Starbucks—

DEAN: Oh, I'm sorry— Should we not have met here?

KENDRA: Oh no! I just can't stomach the stuff. I'm fine.

DEAN: . . . Because of Glor—?

KENDRA: Oh yeah I mean yeah and I realized it makes me anx-
ious which is probably related because you know. When
I drink it, it does sort of remind me of where I was.

DEAN: Sorry— We can totally go somewhere else.

KENDRA: No no no. If it were that bad I'd have to move. It's
just the taste. Like the same thing happens with Sarah
Tweed now too. I mean, I'm sure you have a million of
these things.

(Beat.)

So where have you even been? For a little while, it was like
the only place I could find you was on TV!

DEAN: Yeah that was all a little intense . . .

KENDRA: I felt so bad for you! It was like I couldn't change a
channel without seeing that same footage of you over and
over getting carried out of the lobby—

DEAN *(Embarrassed)*: God—where I'd pissed / myself—

KENDRA: And then all those interviews you had to do about
Gloria and her stupid party and what she said to you—
having to recount it over and over . . . I'm glad it died down.

DEAN: Me, too.

KENDRA: But, oh my god, wait. Happy Birthday!

DEAN: Ha ha oh god, it was—

KENDRA: / Happy Belated Birthday!

DEAN: It was actually three months ago, but thanks.

KENDRA: Thirty—OMG! Did you get to have a . . . party or something?

DEAN: Not really. I spent it with my parents at their house. / And some friends from home.

KENDRA: Aww, that's right, you're from—that's adorable.

DEAN: Yeah. But I'm definitely ready to get the eff out of Jersey.

KENDRA: Wait— You moved back to New Jersey?

DEAN *(After a beat)*: You didn't know about this?

KENDRA: Know about what?

DEAN: Well, after Gloria and the media stuff, I had sort of a breakdown and had to be hospitalized—

KENDRA: Oh my god, Dean—

DEAN: Don't worry— It wasn't for very long— I can't believe you didn't hear about this—

KENDRA: No. Are you . . .

DEAN: Am I . . . ?

KENDRA: Are you doing better?—

DEAN: Oh yeah— But while I was in there my parents came and packed up all of my stuff, and then it wasn't until I was home for a month that they finally told me that they had contacted my landlord and broke my lease, and it was just a fucking nightmare—

KENDRA: Oh no!

DEAN: A fucking nightmare. It was like being kidnapped.

(Beat.)

But I'm actually in the process of moving back—though moving back to New York in your thirties is The Worst. I'm still trying to find a place.

KENDRA: Oh god— Well I'll certainly keep my ears out for any leads.

DEAN: That's nice of you.

KENDRA: Though what am I talking about? With that advance you got, I mean, you could just hire a broker.

(Beat.)

DEAN *(Modest)*: Yeah, well . . .

KENDRA: You know, I just found out about the bidding war. Wait, where did you wind up again? I forget.

DEAN: HarperCollins . . . It was not my first choice, but I was in the hospital during the auction so my agent went with whoever offered the most—

(Beat.)

Anyway, how have you been? You left the magazine?

KENDRA: I actually left like two weeks after—after you—

DEAN: I can't even believe they reopened.

KENDRA: I know. How disgusting was that? But, you know, I was having lunch with Eleanor last week and she says the place is a disaster. Everyone is either new and stressed-out or just traumatized. She gives it a year.

DEAN: You're still in touch with Eleanor? That's nice.

KENDRA: Yeah . . . How about Nan? Are you two—

DEAN: We email.

(Beat.)

Anyway. So what are you doing now?

KENDRA: Oh, just some freelancing.

DEAN: Really?

KENDRA: Yeah . . .

DEAN: I thought I heard somewhere you got a book deal?

(Beat.)

KENDRA: Oh, yes. Well, that, too. But that literally just happened. Wait, how did you hear about it?

DEAN: A little birdy. Called the internet.

(Beat.)

But FSG is a great fit for you. How far along are you?

KENDRA: Well, I just started, so . . .

DEAN: Right.

KENDRA: But what about you?

DEAN *(Gesturing vaguely out the window)*: I literally just came from a meeting with my editor and got about a million notes even though I'm not even finished yet. But they're trying to rush it into print, so . . .

KENDRA: They are?

DEAN: Yeah. Next summer.

KENDRA: And is it still called *'Zine Dreams*?

DEAN: No. I changed / the title.

KENDRA *(With a laugh)*: Thank god— To what?

DEAN: Uh . . . *Gloria*, weirdly enough . . . Their idea.

KENDRA: Not that weird . . . Is Gloria a big . . . part of it, or?—

DEAN: No, no—or I mean, not exactly—or not entirely. It's still a memoir technically—but obviously it ends with her. And there's stuff about our . . . interactions woven throughout.

KENDRA: And you're okay with that?

DEAN: Well, I can't not be okay with it. It's my life.

KENDRA: I'm sorry. I'm happy for you—I'm just suffering from a bit of Gloria fatigue. Isn't it so creepy how in the wake of something like that all people can care about is the perpetrator? It's like, people, why are we giving her what she wants? This sort of attention is obviously why she did it. Like all that terrible stuff about her alcoholic dad and his pistol collection. As if there was actually more to say than that she was a psychopath with a gun? I mean what about the eight people she shot and maimed—not to mention the ten she killed, right? Maybe it's worth telling their stories.

KENDRA: Yes, I remember this from your proposal.

KENDRA: Excuse me?

DEAN: Isn't your whole concept like a focus on the victims, or something? A chapter per victim? Am I just making that up?

(Beat.)

KENDRA: You read my proposal?

DEAN: I did.

KENDRA: On the internet?

DEAN: No, no. A different birdy. At FSG.

(Beat.)

But you have nothing to worry about. It's really strong. Very tight. And your sample chapters? So moving. Especially that chapter on Miles and his family. And Ani. I have to admit I was kind of blown away. I have just never seen you write like that.

KENDRA: Not like I ever had the chance . . .

DEAN: True. Though I always liked your various Twitters.

(Beat.)

Are you writing about me?

(Beat.)

KENDRA: Excuse me?

DEAN: Are you?

KENDRA: Uh, don't flatter yourself . . . Are you writing about me?

(Beat.)

DEAN: Well, I mean, it's a memoir.

KENDRA: Uh-huh. And what have you written?

DEAN: Nothing really . . . Yet.

(Beat.)

It's actually been a weird experience trying to write this. Do you know, I've actually blacked out most of that day?

KENDRA: You did?

DEAN: I can only seem to recall it in bits and pieces—and putting it all together has really forced me to reflect a lot on that time and myself and who I was . . . back then . . . before Gloria, and I've kind of come to this conclusion that maybe I wasn't . . . the best guy . . . that I was an asshole basically—which might have something to do with that environment—but also you know I was drinking a lot and sort of unhappy with where I was in my life and only kind of realizing this—and, anyway, it's just, it has all kind of led me to this place of really wanting to apologize to you . . . for anything I might have said that hurt your feelings or anything like that—

KENDRA: You don't have to do this.

DEAN: No, but I want to.

(Beat.)

Also, I guess, I feel like it is one thing to have felt—or still feel!—however we felt-slash-feel towards each other, but I guess it would be another thing if these feelings sort of . . . found their way into our work. Do you know what I mean? Since we're both writing about that time and that place—

KENDRA: What could I possibly have to write about you, Dean? That you were a mediocre assistant with a drinking problem?

DEAN: I don't know, Kendra. It's not my book. *(Starts going through his bag)* I think it would just be a good idea if we bury the hatchet, if there even is a hatchet. Because who wants, like, a literary feud, right? And it might be nice to actually be watching out for each other, you know, as we both embark on this new chapter in our lives.

KENDRA: Sure, Dean.

DEAN: Okay great!

(Beat.)

Because there's this weird thing . . .

(Dean pushes a small stack of pages toward Kendra.)

KENDRA: Uh, what is this . . . ?

DEAN: It's a little something that my lawyer and agents drafted up and I guess it's something they want us to both sign.

KENDRA: Saying what?

DEAN: It's a kind of nondisclosure agreement? But I guess it's totally a formality at this point, since you're not writing about me.

(Beat.)

KENDRA: Dean, this is crazy. I'm not signing this.

DEAN: Oh no no no, you can take it home, if you want— / Show your—

KENDRA: Dean, I'm not signing this.

DEAN: But you just said you're not writing about me.

(Beat.)

KENDRA: Obviously I am writing about you, Dean.

(Beat.)

After Gloria, you're the freaking face of the tragedy. It's unavoidable. Every news item features you / or quotes you or—

DEAN: Right, but I don't think this says you can't write about me. I think it's more about what you write about me. And, if you read it, you'll see it cuts both ways— We each basically get approval over how we appear / in the other's—

KENDRA: Are you insane? You are not going to tell me what I can and can't write.

(Beat.)

You don't, like, own this experience, Dean. You are aware of that?

DEAN: With all due respect, Kendra, don't I? Or at least a little more than you. You weren't there. You were at Starbucks. Nothing happened to you.

KENDRA: But everything happened to you?

DEAN: Were Miles's last words to you? How about Ani's? Do you know the sound she made between the first and second bullet? Does that sound keep you up at night? Or what about Gloria? Do you know what the look in a person's eyes is like right before they shoot themselves in the face? No. I didn't think so. But this is my lived experience, my actual life and I just can't have you tarnishing it with your—with your—

KENDRA: With my what?

DEAN: With your ambition, Kendra—your greed. I cannot have you . . . profiting from my . . . trauma.

KENDRA: Your trauma? You think I wasn't affected by this?

DEAN: How?!

KENDRA: Do you know what it was like to stand outside that building and see them cart away body bag after body bag and not know who was inside? I lost friends, Dean!

(Beat.)

DEAN: Kendra, are you really going to sit here and tell me you actually considered any of these people "friends"? You made no secret of what you thought of that place or how much better you thought you were than everybody else. You tore apart everyone's work behind their backs. We were all either competition to you—or, worse, just an audience to the tragedy of your thwarted talents. Ani and I were the only people who would put up with you and that's because we had to. And, honestly, if you hadn't excused yourself to Starbucks, Gloria would have killed you.

(Beat.)

KENDRA: But she didn't. And here we are: the survivors.

(Beat.)

So what's the threat here? If I don't sign this thing, you're going to like "defame" me in your memoir? You'll say that I was competitive—that I thought I was better than you? Go ahead. I wasn't there to be liked. I was there to be a writer.

DEAN: What I'll say is that you're writing an exploitative book / in order to save your non-career—

KENDRA: "Exploitative"?

DEAN: You are not some sort of investigative journalist! No one is asking you to write this! There is nothing that qualifies you to write it. And, honestly, I think you know this, which is why you're bending over backwards with this crap concept about "victims." You are not a victim. You are just a leech—a parasite, and these "victims" to you are nothing but an excuse to pad a portfolio of blogging about dresses.

KENDRA: A very bad thing happened to both of us!—to all of us!—yet you seem to think it happened only to you. Why is that? Because you went to Gloria's dumb party and she saved you? Because you were "a witness" to everyone's last moments? Because you're entitled enough to think the world automatically cares about you and what *you* feel and what you saw? And why is that? You did not survive some holocaust.

DEAN: You don't know what I survived.

(Beat.)

KENDRA: I mean, you are aware that the rest of the world has moved on from Gloria, correct? And it's still moving. Every week there's another tragedy, Dean. Every other week there's another disgruntled somebody mowing down a movie theater or a shopping mall or a kindergarten or a doctor's office. With every bullet that passes through another chamber of another gun, Gloria recedes further and further into memory, becomes a shorter and shorter sentence in the annals of American violence. The only thing anyone will probably remember about that day is that Sarah Tweed died.

(Beat.)

So what makes you think that anyone cares about what you saw? I mean, what is the endgame here for you, Dean? Do you honestly believe an actual writing career is waiting for you? A career as what? A "memoirist"? Do you think we're still in the same race?

(Beat.)

DEAN: You know, I haven't written my ending yet. And this will make an interesting scene.

KENDRA: Have you really been sitting here this whole time thinking about the scene this would make—how you would write this all down?! God, this is so sad. Gloria thought she was saving your life, but there was no life there to save. What was all that worth now, Dean? All that networking? All that self-righteousness? All that slaving away in that cubicle being Nan's lapdog? Was it worth it? Your fifteen minutes as a footnote in the life of the office psycho?

DEAN: Be careful you don't wind up in my book.

KENDRA: Be careful your book doesn't wind up in my book!

(Beat.)

Don't you see it's over, Dean? Every breath you've taken—every dream you've dreamt—Gloria took it. It's hers now! They're even renaming your memoir *Gloria*. I mean, maybe it's time to wake up. Maybe those *'Zine Dreams* are dead. Maybe life means nothing now. Your life means nothing. Cut your losses and start over.

(Dean reaches across the table and slaps Kendra across the face. Shawn reacts.)

SHAWN: / Whoa! Hey! Hey!

DEAN: There's your violence, you bitch! Don't tell me my life means nothing! / You don't know what it was like! You don't know what it was like!

SHAWN: Hey, man! Stop! Stop! Take that out of here!

(Dean starts to gather his things.)

KENDRA *(Shouting after him, taunting)*: No. But I know what that was like. And I know how my book ends!

SHAWN *(To Dean)*: You gotta get out of here! Get out of here!

(Dean exits. Shawn makes sure he's gone. Kendra seems genuinely freaked-out but tries to hold it together. She pulls a notebook out of her purse and writes something down.)

What was that? Are you okay?

KENDRA: I'm fine. Do you have ice? I think I need ice.

SHAWN *(Getting her ice)*: Do you want me to call somebody or—
KENDRA: No.
SHAWN: Well maybe you should just stay in here for a little bit just in case. *(Beat, looking out)* Who was that?
KENDRA: Nobody.
SHAWN: Really? I thought he looked familiar.
KENDRA: Just a crazy person.
SHAWN: Maybe I just knew he was gonna be trouble. Sometimes you can just tell, man. You can just sense it when they walk in. Dudes can't be hitting on females. That's not right.

(Nan—who looks a lot like Gloria—walks in with Sasha, an editor at a nearby publishing house and former assistant—who looks a lot like Ani. Sasha is in the middle of greeting Shawn, when Nan sees Kendra.)

SASHA *(To Shawn)*: Hi.
NAN *(To Sasha)*: Wait a second. *(To Kendra)* Kendra?

(Kendra wheels around, sees Nan, not sure if it's her. Beat, in which she doesn't say anything for a long time.)

KENDRA: N—Nan?
NAN: What a surprise! Wait, did I just see Dean on the street?
KENDRA: Yeah— We just had coffee.
NAN: Oh!
KENDRA: What are / you doing here?
NAN *(To Sasha)*: That was Dean! *(To Kendra)* Long-standing coffee date. That is so great that you two are still in touch.
SHAWN *(To Sasha)*: / Can I start your order?
KENDRA: Yes!
SASHA: / Yes. I'll have a skim macchiato with extra foam.
KENDRA: How are things at the magazine?
NAN: Oh, I actually left about a month ago.
KENDRA: You did? For where?

SHAWN: / Anything else?

NAN (*Opening her jacket, revealing*): Well, I'm pregnant—

KENDRA: Oh! / Oh wow!

NAN: Yes. Eight months. And it's twins.

SASHA: Excuse me—Nan? Can I get you something?

NAN (*Moving for her wallet*): Oh, I can—

SASHA: Stop— It's on us.

NAN: Just tea. Chamomile.

SASHA (*To Kendra, being polite*): Hi.

NAN: Oh, this is Sasha Leven / son—

KENDRA: Yes, I totally know / who this is!

NAN: Oh, okay. I didn't know you already—

KENDRA: Hi. You used to work at the magazine.

(Sasha gives Kendra a tight smile.)

SASHA (*To Shawn*): And a venti chamomile, / please.

NAN: Anyway, it was time. And I wanted to see what this kind of life might be like.

KENDRA: Yes. And that work-motherhood balance can be so difficult.

NAN: Uh-huh . . . Plus the atmosphere there was getting a little toxic.

(Beat.)

KENDRA: Well, we should do lunch or something soon?

NAN (*Sort of cagey*): Oh—

KENDRA: Or, like a coffee maybe, or something—

NAN: Of course. Let me— Will you just email me? My schedule's crazy but—

KENDRA: Totally.

NAN: You can get my email from Dean.

(Beat.)

Well . . . I have to get my drink now.

KENDRA: Right! I've got to go, too! It was nice running into you.

NAN: You, too.

KENDRA: Bye!

SASHA: Bye bye.

(Kendra exits.)

NAN: Good god.

SASHA: Who was that?

NAN: Eleanor Gardner's old assistant. Kendra Something. Did you overlap with her?

SASHA: No, but she was a little aggressive . . .

NAN: Yes. Eleanor used to refer to her as her "Tiger Daughter."

SASHA: Oh no—isn't that a little offensive?

NAN: Calling her a tiger?

SASHA: Yeah, like that whole "Tiger Mom" thing, or—?

NAN: Oh! Oh right. Wow I never put that together . . . I thought tigers were from Africa? You know what? Never mind. Eleanor's great—she's just old. The point is that she was afraid of her. I once asked Eleanor why she didn't just fire the girl and she told me she was too scared that if she fired her, Kendra would just climb the ladder somewhere else and come back to haunt her. Called her an ambition junkie. And Eleanor would know. I mean, she's been in the business so long, she's seen every type of anybody that has ever passed through this world. And she was right. I mean, the girl just sold some book on Gloria and she wasn't even there.

SHAWN *(Setting out a drink)*: Skim macchiato / extra foam.

SASHA: Oh that was Kendra Park!

NAN: —Yes.

SASHA: How many more books about Gloria can that place take?

NAN: She sat in the cubicle right next to Dean, too.

SASHA: Poor Dean— You know, we actually tried to bid on his book—

NAN: You did?

SASHA: Yes, though they were just these sample pages from a memoir he'd been shopping around—did you ever see them?

NAN: Of course I did—

SASHA: Just terrible, right? And the whole thing was so icky with his little agent holding that auction less than a week after the shooting. But I just was trying to be supportive because, of course, I knew him and I spent the whole time thinking, "It could have been me in that cubicle!" You know?

NAN: Did you know Gloria?

SASHA: Of course I knew Gloria. Didn't you?

NAN: Actually, Sasha, I barely knew the woman. Isn't that terrible? And, apparently, Gloria and I were the exact same age and we'd started around the same time. I mean, we must have worked on something together at some point but I usually request Christine.

SHAWN *(Setting out another drink)*: Venti chamomile.

SASHA *(Retrieving her drink)*: Thanks, Shawn.

NAN: Ugh—I want to talk about something else. Let's sit by the window.

(Beat.)

How are things at—

(Drinks in hand, they find a table.)

SASHA: Fine. You know: it's books. People kind of still read them. Kind of. Sort of. Oprah fucked us. E-readers fucked us. Amazon continues to fuck us. And now this new publisher's trying to push this new acquisition model, where all we try to do is get things that someone will want to option for a movie so that it will be turned into a movie so that we can get the book sales. So we make books that feel like movies. I feel a little screwed. I got into this business to make books I really cared about—that spoke to me and my generation. Now half my list is YA crossover—

(Dean crosses in front of the window.)

NAN: Is that Dean?

(Dean reenters to retrieve the manuscript he left under his seat. Shawn sees Dean, makes a move as if to block him.)

SHAWN: Man, what are you doing?
DEAN: I left something! Relax!
SHAWN: Alright, well where is it? I'll bring it to you.
DEAN: What am I? Like banned from this place?
SHAWN: Yo where is it?
DEAN: It's right there, under the chair—those papers—
NAN: Dean?
DEAN: Nan—
NAN: Is everything okay?
DEAN: Yes, uh—hi!

(Dean makes a move toward Nan. Shawn stops him.)

SHAWN: Hey, come on. Don't do this to me.
DEAN: What, I can't say hi to my fr—my friend?
SHAWN *(Handing over the manuscript)*: Dude, I'm not getting fired for any craziness——
NAN: What is going on?
DEAN *(To Shawn)*: Fine! I'll just stand in the door! Can I do that?! *(To Nan)* Hi, Nan.
NAN *(Seeing something in his face)*: Are you okay?
DEAN: I'm great—

(Beat.)

Is that—is that Sasha?

NAN: Yes! Your old predecessor—

SASHA: Hi, Intern! I barely recognized you with your beard. How are you doing?

DEAN: Good.

SASHA: Are those the proofs for your book?

DEAN: Yes.

SASHA: I'm so looking forward to reading it!

DEAN: Don't hold your breath.

SASHA: Excuse me?

DEAN: I said don't hold your breath. I may be dead—I mean I may die first—I mean I may be dead before I ever finish it. Or maybe I'll burn it.

(Beat.)

What are you guys meeting about?

NAN: Oh we're . . . just catching up—

DEAN *(To Sasha)*: I've been trying to get a coffee with this one for months. You'd think five years would put you at the top of some list but I guess not. *(To Nan)* Did you get any of my emails?

NAN: Yes! Sorry. I'm so behind. But you know— *(Gestures to her stomach)* Life is so hard without a superstar assistant!

(Beat.)

. . . But we ran into Kendra!

DEAN: You did?

NAN: She says you two reconnected?

(Beat.)

DEAN: Tell me what to do.

NAN: I'm sorry?

DEAN: About my book. You're an editor. How do I fix it? How do I rethink it? How do I un-think it? What do I do—

(Dean has a panic attack, falls to the floor.)

NAN: Dean! What's going on?
DEAN *(Getting up)*: I'm fine. I have to go. I have to go.
NAN: Oh, uh, okay—
DEAN: I'll talk to you.

(Dean exits.)

SASHA: Should I not have brought up the book?
NAN: What do I do? Do I go after him?
SASHA: No no no—
NAN *(To Shawn)*: Why wouldn't you let him in?
SHAWN: He slapped that girl earlier.
NAN: The one who was just here?
SHAWN: Yeah.
NAN: Oh my / god.
SASHA: He slapped her? *(Off Shawn's nod)* She didn't seem slapped!

(Nan has a moment.)

Nan, are you okay?
NAN: What do I do, Sasha?
SASHA: This is my fault. Do you want to go somewhere else? I should have known we would run into everybody here. Or do you want to reschedule?
NAN: No, no. I just need a minute.

(Beat.)

I mean, he's right. I've been ignoring his emails but I just haven't had room in my life for—for that! I'm pregnant, for crying out loud. I have a family on the way. So. But it was also five years we spent together. He knows some of my habits and quirks better than David does and I also feel like I've . . . watched him grow up somehow—I just feel so guilty.

(Beat.)

It's just so hard to watch—when something like this comes out of nowhere and just derails your . . . just derails everything. I just wish things would go back—to the way they were. And not just for him. But for me too. I mean, I was on the other side of the glass when the woman blew her brains out!

SASHA: Oh god—I didn't know—!

NAN: And I'd just been talking to our intern, who she shot like five minutes after he left my office— Did you ever hear anything about him?

SASHA: What? No?

NAN: Oh, it's actually the saddest story. Somehow he's been, like, completely just written out of the whole thing. His name was Mark. One of Richard Morrison's students? He was this incredibly bright kid. Black. Harvard. Anyway, it was going to be his last day working with us—

SASHA: Oh my god.

NAN: I know. And anyway he did that thing, where he asked to meet with me before he left, which was so sweet—

SASHA: Oh I love when they do that.

NAN: Me, too, but you know, sometimes it can backfire. And I wasn't completely expecting him to be a suck-up, but I did brace myself. But then he came in and sat down. I asked him how he had enjoyed his experience, and then he told me that it had just been, "Okay."

SASHA: What?

NAN: And, of course, I was like, "Tell me more." And what I realized is that Richard Morrison had filled this poor boy's head with all these stories about how fun the office used to be, how crazy it was back in the day, and he'd been disappointed. Of course, he was talking about the time back when they had martini carts making the rounds every day at four and there were always these illicit affairs happening all over the office and coke being done in bathrooms and all sorts of other hijinks, and yes, I guess that exact historical time did sort of . . . produce . . . the most interesting work? But it was also—

SASHA: Pre-internet.

NAN: Yes, well, I was going to say a disaster, but, yes, pre-internet, too, I suppose.

SASHA: Well, there was no internet. When you sat at your desk, you had no choice but to work. And then when you were done working, you went crazy.

NAN: Yes but it was also a financial disaster—mostly because everyone was walking around with these substance-abuse problems —and that's half the reason why we went corporate the way we did—got bought out—we were so in the red. But anyway, Mark was saying, basically, that he thought he was going to be somewhere that was . . . more charged, more vibrant . . . and he found it lacking. And he told me some story Richard had told him about his early days there and it was a funny story—god, what was it? It was a story I actually knew, because I was there and now I can't remember it—it'll come to me —but, anyway, it was a funny story, a funny story for him I guess but it was a memory for me—and it was strange to feel your experience come back to you that way, a story in some young person's mouth. And we were laughing about it. We were both laughing over this thing that he'd only heard about and this thing that I'd actually lived through and it was . . . weird. And then, almost as suddenly, the laughing stopped and—it was like he was reading my mind when he asked me, "What happened?" And I didn't know what else to say except, "Things were different then. Everyone was young and didn't know what they were doing. Everything was new and exciting and always discovery. And then it got old. We got old. And now things are different." And it was quiet for a moment and we talked about a few more things, all the while I'm thinking, "Did I really just say that?" And he got up, and just before he left I found myself blurting out, "If you ever want a career in publishing . . ." Just like that. And I knew that it was me, like, trying to convince myself that he was young and naive and that I was wise and the one with all the power. But he just looked at me with the saddest, most knowing look on his face, and just thanked me and left. Then, five minutes later, Gloria happened. I'd just seen the email from Bo when I heard those gunshots and those screams and before I knew what was happening, I was underneath that desk. He was dead. And then I realized I was pregnant—

SASHA: What?!

NAN: I just put it together. I'd been vomiting all morning and I had missed my period but I'm so stressed all the time missing a period isn't even a—okay, TMI—but flash-forward, I'm underneath my desk, trying not to breathe, afraid I would make some sort of noise and it took me some minutes to realize I was clutching my belly. That was where my hands went. Straight over my stomach. And I was thinking to myself, "Who did this? Who put those hands there?" It was like some part of me was already working, without my even noticing it. It was like some part of me had already made the decision without my conscious self even noticing it. And I just kept thinking, "Who did this? Did I do this? Did I do this?"

(Beat.)

I was under that desk for hours—

SASHA: What?

NAN: Yeah, everyone else got out pretty much as soon as it was over—I mean the whole thing must have taken fifteen minutes—but I didn't know what was going on—

I didn't know it was over, and, you know, just my luck Gloria decides to end her killing spree right in front of my
office. She kills herself right there in front of my door.
There were three bodies less than ten feet away from me,
blood everywhere. I could see it, all over the glass. And
I just couldn't open the door. I just refused. I just sat and
my whole life just flashed before my eyes and all I could
think of was the intern, our conversation.

(Beat.)

Eventually, I came to my senses and called 911 and the
police found me. They cleared a path and walked me
out with a coat over my head and it was a nightmare.
My shoes kept slipping on the . . . Anyway, that's when
I black out. The next thing I know, I'm sitting on my couch
with my husband, watching all these news reports about
this woman I barely knew shooting up the office I'd been
working my entire adult life and there's my assistant being
carried away, and it was suddenly like I didn't recognize
anything— or anyone —anymore, including myself, not
my new self or my old self—I did not recognize the person
I'd been for the last however many years and I did not
know the person sitting on that couch watching TV with
my husband except that I knew that that was the real me.
It was like some spell had broken and I still don't know if
it was a good or a bad thing. But it's totally changed me.
I feel . . . different.

(Beat.)

SASHA: Nan! Where did that just come from?
NAN: What?
SASHA: This story! How have you never considered turning this
    into something?
NAN: Into what?

SASHA: Uh, a book?

NAN: Oh come on, I thought you said everyone was sick of stories about Gloria—

SASHA: Well, yes, for a bunch of twenty-somethings writing about it. I mean, for them, you know—and my heart really does go out to all of them; no one should have to go through something like this—but this is like the only real thing that's ever happened to them. No wonder they're all scrambling to get it down on paper. But you've got experience. You've witnessed things and, unlike them, Gloria is not the defining center of your being. She's the backdrop to a very real, very human, I might even say, spiritual realization about time passage and motherhood and mortality. These are things that people—real people—can connect to.

(Beat.)

NAN: Do you really think there's something there?

SASHA: Yes.

NAN: You know, I had actually been wondering . . .

(Beat.)

What do you think I could get?

(Blackout.
  Bach's Mass in B Minor *continues.)*

Scene Two

Years later.

  The office of a film and television production company somewhere in Los Angeles.

  A cluster of two cubicles. One is empty, the other is occupied by Callie—who looks a lot like Ani and Sasha—who sits reading a manuscript. She is rapt and a little emotional, dabbing occasionally at her eyes with a ball of tissue. She reads and emotes for a stretch before Rashaad—who looks a lot like Miles—enters with his new employee, Lorin. It is a little awkward between them, but Lorin is in surprisingly good spirits.

RASHAAD: And so that's basically the tour.

LORIN: Cool.

  (Beat.)

RASHAAD *(Indicating the cubicle next to Callie)*: And here's where you'll sit.

LORIN: Okay, great.

(Beat.)

RASHAAD *(Indicating a nearby door)*: And my office is here.

LORIN: Okay.

RASHAAD: Cool.

(Beat.)

Oh and—just a heads-up—there's not a whole lot to do right now, since we're between cycles, so most of what you'll be doing is answering phones. I hope that's not too weird.

LORIN: Not weird at all. I answer a mean phone.

RASHAAD: Of course.

(Beat.)

I'm sorry and can you remind me your name again?

LORIN: Lorin.

RASHAAD: That's right. Lorin. Lorin, Lorin, Lorin. Forgive me. I'm just—I'm completely terrible with names—I'm good with faces—just terrible with names. *(Beat, then indicating)* Alright! So my office is—

LORIN: Right.

RASHAAD: You can just knock if you need anything. I'll see if I can rustle up some scripts for you to read. It might be good for you to get to know some of what we're working on, I guess?

LORIN: Totally.

RASHAAD: Alright. I'll print them out and . . .

(Rashaad gestures to a printer.)

LORIN: Okeydoke.

(With an awkward smile, Rashaad disappears into his office and slides the door closed. Lorin notices Callie. He stares a while before:)

Hi.

(Callie doesn't respond, absorbed as she is in the manuscript. Lorin sort of takes that as a cue to sit down and mind his own business. He turns on the computer at his desk and stares at Callie for a while as it loads. She reminds him of someone. She eventually feels him staring at her and looks up. They meet eyes.)

Hi.

(Callie doesn't say anything, looks so disturbed, forces a smile, goes back to reading. He looks around for what he should do. Lorin watches her read for a bit, thinking about Ani, before he realizes that his computer has loaded. He tries to log in and fails.)

Hey, I'm sorry, but do you know what the log-in is for this computer?

(Beat.)

CALLIE *(Sounding on the verge of tears)*: I.T. was just here to set it up. He'll be right back.
LORIN: Okay . . .

(For lack of anything better to do, Lorin settles in, takes out his headphones and his phone, and checks his mail or something. Eventually, Callie finishes the manuscript she's reading and puts it to the side, sits back, and heaves a satisfied sigh.)

CALLIE *(Small, to herself)*: Oh my god.

(Beat, in which she stews in her feelings, blows her nose, tries to pull herself together.)

LORIN: Are you okay?

CALLIE: Yes. Hi. Sorry. I was just like—

(She gestures to the manuscript.)

LORIN: No problem.

CALLIE: You're Rashaad's new assistant.

LORIN: Uh, I guess . . . Lorin.

CALLIE: Callie.

(They shake hands.)

So weird right? He looks like he's, like, nineteen?

LORIN: Who?

CALLIE: Rashaad.

LORIN: Oh—ha—a little bit, yeah.

CALLIE: He just got promoted. Like two weeks ago, he was an assistant—and he was sitting right there where you're sitting. Then he started optioning people's Tinder profiles and now he's a VP and it's like what the fuck is even happening right now? But I mean like there is all this turnover here, so what can you do? I just wish he wasn't, like, being so gross about it—I mean, like his hiring you— What a douche move, right?

LORIN: Well—

CALLIE: I mean, no offense—but you could almost be his dad, right? It's such a power trip. So annoying.

(Beat.)

LORIN: I'm not that old.

CALLIE: I mean—you know what I mean.

LORIN: Yeah, well, I wasn't exactly "hired." I'm a temp.

CALLIE: Ohhhhhhhhhhhhhhhhhhhh! Oh oh oh oh—

LORIN: I was just placed here until, I guess, he . . . finds someone more permanent.

CALLIE: Oh! Oh, okay. They might hire you! That's happened before. Are you interested in film or television?

LORIN: Not really. I'm just doing this while I prep for the LSATs.

CALLIE: Okay. How long are you here, do you know?

LORIN: Just a month. I think.

CALLIE: That's good! Maybe you'll like it so much you'll wanna stay?

LORIN: How long have you been here?

CALLIE: Coming up on two years.

LORIN: Nice. You like it here.

CALLIE: Oh, yeah, I love it. I'm a big book nerd and my boss does book options, so, I basically just get to read a lot of stuff before it comes out. It's nice.

LORIN: Yeah, looks like you were in it just now.

CALLIE: Oh? Oh yeah, I'm just doing coverage, but this is actually an amazing book. Remember those terrible shootings that happened at that magazine like . . . years ago?

LORIN: Yeah. Very well actually.

CALLIE: Ugh, I know—I was obsessed— But this is like someone's memoir about it?

LORIN: Is that *Gloria*?

CALLIE: Oh no—but I read that one. I thought it was, like, kind of pretentious and had no story. What did you think?

LORIN: I didn't read it.

CALLIE: Oh. Well, I, you're not missing anything. And didn't it come out later that the girl who wrote it was like in a Starbucks or something when it happened? Anyway, this one is like a million times better—

LORIN: Who wrote it?

CALLIE (*Checking the book*): Uh . . . Nancy Martin?

LORIN: You're fucking kidding me? Nan Martin wrote a memoir about Gloria?

CALLIE: You know her?

LORIN: I kind of know all those people.

CALLIE: You do?!

LORIN: Yeah. I worked there. I was there when it happened . . . Gloria.

CALLIE: No way!

LORIN: Yes way.

CALLIE: Oh my god! Oh my god!

(Beat.)

LORIN *(Referring to the manuscript)*: Do you think I'm, like, in it?

CALLIE: I—I don't know—

LORIN: Can I see that?

CALLIE *(Handing it over)*: Yes. Of course! Oh my god.

(Beat.)

You know, she's coming here in like fifteen minutes for like a meeting?

LORIN: Nan?

(Callie nods.)

Wait— Are you guys making a show out of this?

CALLIE: Uh, well, we have the film rights.

LORIN: You do?

CALLIE: But the feature guy who handled them left and my boss thinks we should pitch it as a limited series.

LORIN *(Flipping through it)*: What the shit! Why? Why is it so good?

CALLIE: Well, I mean, it's just a very well-written, very, like, moving personal story and, um, basically, she has this amazing frame where she's underneath her desk and you don't totally know why, but then you realize that the shooting is happening, and it all takes place inside of her head during like the two hours she had to be under the desk, because she didn't even know when the shooting was over. And, so basically her entire life is flashing before her eyes underneath this desk and you just hear about, like, all of these sacrifices that she had to make and how she'd, like, started to hate herself and then, basically, in the end, she looks down and she realizes that she's been clutching her stomach for like two hours and reveals that she just figured out she's pregnant, basically, with, like, twins? And she's forty. And she realizes that she, like, has to have these babies if she gets out of here, and so then there's, like, all this tension about how she may never get out alive? And it's just basically about how, like, wherever, like, death and chaos lurk, there's also, like, life? And that that is basically the human experience? It's just so emotional.

LORIN: God, that is such crap. Nan was a total ice queen.

CALLIE: Really?

LORIN: Yeah. And she was an editor. The editors didn't even, like, see anything.

CALLIE: Really?

LORIN: Yeah. Someone saw Gloria loading the guns in the supply closet and went to tell the managing editor who sent out an email to all the editors telling them to lock their doors and stay inside, because the glass surrounding their offices was apparently bulletproof or shatterproof or something?

CALLIE: Whoa.

(Beat.)

How did you survive?

LORIN: Uh, I . . . saw people running so . . . I ran, too.

CALLIE: Oh . . .

(Jenna, Callie's boss, pokes her head out of her office—she looks a lot like Kendra.)

JENNA: Callie! What is going on? I need that coverage!

CALLIE *(Gathering manuscripts)*: Sorry, Jenna—I finished but I got distracted. I can totally tell you what it's about.

JENNA: Fine. *(To Lorin)* Hi.

LORIN: Hi

JENNA *(Flirtatious)*: Are you Rashaad's new assistant?

LORIN: Sort of—I'm temping.

JENNA: Ahhhhh—I see.

(Beat.)

Well, welcome.

LORIN: Thanks.

(Jenna and Callie exit into Jenna's office. The door slides closed. Meanwhile, Devin, the I.T. guy—who looks a lot like Dean—enters.)

DEVIN: Hey. Somebody need I.T.?

LORIN: Oh, yeah, hi. I'm Lorin.

DEVIN *(Gets to work on Lorin's computer)*: Hey. Devin.

(Devin works on Lorin's computer.)

LORIN *(Making conversation)*: Is everyone who works here, like, twelve?

DEVIN: I know, right? Where you here from?

LORIN: I just moved back from New York. I'm actually from here.

(Jenna and Callie reenter from Jenna's office. Jenna goes straight up to Lorin.)

JENNA: I'm sorry. Callie just told me everything. You were there?

LORIN: Yeah.

CALLIE *(Crushing on Devin)*: Hey, Devin!

JENNA: Do you know Nancy Martin? We're meeting her in, like, ten minutes!

LORIN: I mean, we worked together for a long time—

JENNA: That is nuts! Did you know we're meeting her in, like, ten minutes?

(Rashaad comes out of his office.)

RASHAAD: Guys, could you keep it down? I'm watching something.

JENNA: Uh, did you know your new assistant worked at that magazine where that lady shot everyone?

RASHAAD: From Untitled Gloria Project? Oh snap.

(The phone on Callie's desk buzzes.)

JENNA: Oh my god—is that her? That's her!

CALLIE *(Into the phone)*: Yes. Hi. I'll come get her. *(Hangs up)* It's her.

(Callie exits.)

JENNA: How long has it been since you've seen each other?

LORIN: Yeah, not since it / hap—

JENNA: This is going to be crazy! What are you going to say?

LORIN: I don't—I don't know—

RASHAAD: Wait, where is Marketing? We should Vimeo this— no, Facebook Live it—no, TikTok—

JENNA: Wait— Did you know the shooter, too?

LORIN: Gloria? Yeah, I guess . . .

JENNA: Really? We've been dying for someone to tell us about her, but, like, nobody seemed to really know her.

LORIN: That's not true. She'd been there a long time. A lot of people knew her.

RASHAAD: What about the guy who was her best friend? The one she saved? Did you know him too?

LORIN: Dean wasn't her best friend!!

JENNA: Didn't he have a memoir, but it never materialized? What happened with that?

LORIN: Uh—

JENNA: Do you know if he ever finished it?

RASHAAD: Hey, Jenna? Let's have one question at a time? Lorin, sorry, dude. Do you know what packaging is?

(Lorin shakes his head.)

No. Okay, packaging is when we take a movie star and attach them to a script in order to add value to it to make it more attractive to networks, but movie stars want juicy roles, right? So they can win awards, right? And Gloria is a juicy role, right? So, if we were going to cast Gloria today, who would you approach? I mean, it could literally be any star. Nicole Kidman. Reese Witherspoon. Dream big.

LORIN: Gloria? A star? I don't know . . .

RASHAAD: Okay . . . How about you give us some sense of her qualities?

LORIN: I don't know—she was pretty normal? Like maybe a little awkward?

JENNA: A little awkward?

LORIN: Just shy. She kept to herself.

RASHAAD: Okay, that's good. What else can you tell us about her?

LORIN: I don't know— She was from, like, Florida?

RASHAAD: Good. Creepy.

LORIN: It wasn't that creepy. She was actually very smart, very well-read. And she could be really nice sometimes—even funny. I mean, she was normal—

JENNA: Okay, you keep saying that, but if she was so normal, then why did she shoot all those people? That's normal?

LORIN: I just think people have really exaggerated her . . . personality . . . I don't think anything about her, like, screamed killer. I mean, she kept to herself but she was otherwise normal. She read a lot. She always made her own lunch and brought it to work in these little Tupperware containers and the lunches always smelled good when she reheated them in the microwave and they seemed like they took a lot of time to prepare. And she would always offer you some if you asked about them. She spent a lot of time in the fall knitting, so I guess she was crafty. She once knit me a pair of socks when I asked her to. And I was sort of joking but she did it anyway and they lasted a long time and they were really warm. She liked reality TV. She was normal. She did normal things. If anything, she was really just alone at her job, which is fucked-up because the job was her life, and, in some way, I'm not surprised she did what she did. It wasn't the healthiest work environment— Like, it could have been any of us.

(Jenna and Rashaad back away slightly.)

DEVIN: Then why didn't you shoot everyone?

LORIN: I just don't understand why you need to make a movie or a miniseries or whatever of this or cast anything! Like why don't you just make up your own story? Like why do you have to *use* Gloria's?

JENNA: It's not Gloria's story. It's Nan's story.

LORIN: What? No it's not! This was a thing that happened to a lot of people! Not just Nan! Nan didn't see anything! Nan was part of the problem! Nan didn't even know Gloria. Nan probably never even noticed her. And, honestly, if Gloria worked here, if she walked in the door right now, you all probably wouldn't notice her either!

(Callie enters with Nan.)

CALLIE: Here she is . . .

(Beat. Nan clearly has no idea why everyone is standing around, looking at her.)

NAN: Hi.
JENNA: Hi, Nancy.

(Everyone looks at Lorin expectantly.)

LORIN: Hi . . . Nan . . .
NAN *(Clearly not recognizing him)*: Hi?

(Beat.)

CALLIE: Don't you guys know each other?
NAN: Do we?
LORIN: I think we used to work together?
NAN: Oh! Oh my god, hi! Remind me your—
LORIN: Lorin.
NAN: Oh! A fact-checker, right? Hello! It's been years! How are you doing?
LORIN: Good.
NAN: It's crazy what happened at the office. With Gloria? Obviously you heard—
LORIN: Yeah. I was there . . .
NAN: Oh! Oh of course! Of course!

(Beat.)

But can you believe it's been two years?
LORIN: Yup. It's all just a memory now.
NAN: Sometimes I think about it and I'm like—did that even happen to me?

(Beat.)

But look at us, huh?

(Beat.)

You're in L.A. now—
LORIN: Yup . . .
NAN: Working in television! How exciting!
LORIN: I'm actually just temping.
NAN *(Disappointed)*: Oh . . .

(Beat.)

Well it's good to see you!
LORIN: Yeah, you, too.

(Beat, in which everyone seems completely underwhelmed.)

DEVIN: Wait, dude! You're a temp?! UGH! Oh . . . my . . . fucking . . . god.

(Devin walks off.)

RASHAAD: That guy always has such a bad attitude!
NAN: So, uh, Jenna—should we start?
JENNA: Oh, yeah. Yes. Do you want anything?
NAN: I would love a coffee.
CALLIE: I was just going to go for a Starbucks run. What do you
want?
NAN: Just a regular coffee. Large. Skim milk.
JENNA: Actually, could you get me an almond-milk cortado with
four shots?
CALLIE: Okay.
JENNA *(To Nan)*: Come on in.

(Jenna and Nan exit into Jenna's office.)

CALLIE *(To Lorin)*: You want anything?

LORIN: No. I'm good.

RASHAAD: Actually I'll take—

CALLIE: Rashaad. You have your own assistant.

(Beat. Rashaad and Lorin awkwardly lock eyes and smile at each other.)

LORIN: I can get you something.

RASHAAD: Uhhhhhhhhhhhhhhhhhhh . . . You know, maybe in a little bit. Let me print you these scripts.

(Rashaad exits back into his office.)

CALLIE *(To Lorin)*: I think Rashaad is like afraid of you. That is hilarious.

(Beat.)

Okay. BRB.

(Callie starts to exit, just as Devin is reentering.)

Hey, Devin, I was just about to make a Starbucks run. Do you want anything?

DEVIN: You know I don't drink that shit.

(Callie exits, as Devin crosses to Lorin's cubicle with a piece of paper.)

No one tells me any fucking thing around here and I wind up looking like an asshole. Okay, so here's the deal. If you're a temp, you don't get your own ID. You get a temp ID. This piece of paper has all your log-in information.

LORIN: Oh. Okay.

DEVIN: That's it?

LORIN: I guess so.

DEVIN *(Starts to exit)*: Good fucking luck at this fucking place!

LORIN: Hey.

(Devin stops.)

Thank you. I really appreciate your help.

DEVIN *(A little taken aback)*: You're welcome.

(Beat.)

LORIN: Hey, do you want to grab a drink sometime, or . . . ?

(Beat.)

DEVIN: Uh. That's really nice of you but I actually have a girl-friend . . .

LORIN: Oh— No! I meant, like, just a beer or something.

DEVIN: Oh! Oh god / sorry—

LORIN: I'm not—

DEVIN: Sorry—

LORIN: I was just curious about I.T.—what's going on around here . . .

(Beat.)

DEVIN: . . . But aren't you just a temp?

LORIN: Yeah, I'm trying this thing out where, like, I wanna know the people I spend my whole day with.

(Beat.)

DEVIN: You know, I'm not gonna, like, shoot up the office.

LORIN: No, no—I'm just trying to be more . . . present or some-thing.

(Beat.)

I just started to be more comfortable around people again. A year ago, I couldn't even step foot in a place like this. I've forgotten how to be . . . in an office.

(Beat.)

DEVIN: Okay. Yeah, sure. Let's get a beer sometime.
LORIN: Cool.
DEVIN: This was so awkward. I'm sorry.
LORIN: No. Don't even worry about it.

(Beat.)

DEVIN: See you later.

(Devin exits. Lorin sits at his desk. He logs into his computer.
Nan's laughter comes from Jenna's office. It annoys Lorin. He tries to ignore it but, eventually, there's more laughter.
Lorin tries to deal with it, but he can't. He puts on his noise-canceling headphones, plugs them into his smartphone. Bach's Mass in B Minor *plays. Lorin hits a button and it switches to the Sarah Tweed song. He turns it up extra loud.*
Meanwhile, the printer next to him churns for a bit, starts to print, stops, and then beeps loudly. Rashaad's door slides open. He seems to be calling for Lorin, but can't be heard over the music.)

RASHAAD: Hey, Lawrence!

(Beat.)

Louis?

(Beat.)

Liam?

(Beat.)

Lars!

(Beat.)

Leonard?

(Beat.)

Lucas?

(Beat.)

Luther?

(Blackout.)

END OF PLAY

BRANDEN JACOBS-JENKINS is a Brooklyn-based writer and award-winning theater artist. His other plays include *Girls*, *Everybody*, *War*, *Appropriate*, *An Octoroon*, and *Neighbors*. He teaches at The University of Texas at Austin.